THE IMPORTANCE OF

Chief Joseph

by
Lois Warburton

Lucent Books, P.O. Box 289011, San Diego, CA 92198-9011

These and other titles are included in The Importance Of
biography series:

Benjamin Franklin
Chief Joseph
Christopher Columbus
Marie Curie
Galileo Galilei
Richard M. Nixon
Jackie Robinson
H.G. Wells

THE IMPORTANCE OF

Chief Joseph

Library of Congress Cataloging-in-Publication Data

Warburton, Lois, 1938–
    Chief Joseph / by Lois Warburton
       p. cm.—(The Importance of)
    Includes bibliographical references and index.
    Summary: A biography of the Nez Percé Indian chief who
led his people in a flight from their Oregon lands to Canada in
1877.
    ISBN 1-56006-030-1 (acid-free pap.)
    1. Joseph, Nez Percé Chief, 1840–1904—Juvenile literature.
2. Nez Percé Indians—History—Juvenile literature. [1. Joseph,
Nez Percé Chief, 1840–1904. 2. Nez Percé Indians—Biography.
3. Indians of North America—Biography.]   I. Title.   II. Series.
E99.N5J678   1992
979'.004974—dc20   92-28010
                                     CIP
                                     AC

Copyright 1992 by Lucent Books, Inc., P.O. Box 289011, San
Diego, California, 92198-9011

Dedication

To Adam and Rachael
Chief Grandchildren

Thanks and Credit to

The author wishes to thank two members of the Nez Percé tribe for their time and cooperation:

Christopher Webb,
Nez Percé Reservation, Lapwai, Idaho; and

Judy Wetan,
Colville Reservation, Nespelem, Washington.

Contents

Foreword

THE IMPORTANCE OF biography series deals with individuals who have made a unique contribution to history. The editors of the series have deliberately chosen to cast a wide net and include people from all fields of endeavor. Individuals from politics, music, art, literature, philosophy, science, sports, and religion are all represented. In addition, the editors did not restrict the series to individuals whose accomplishments have helped change the course of history. Of necessity, this criterion would have eliminated many whose contribution was great, though limited. Charles Darwin, for example, was responsible for radically altering the scientific view of the natural history of the world. His achievements continue to impact the study of science today. Others, such as Chief Joseph of the Nez Percé, played a pivotal role in the history of their own people. While Joseph's influence does not extend much beyond the Nez Percé, his nonviolent resistance to white expansion and his continuing role in protecting his tribe and his homeland remain an inspiration to all.

These biographies are more than factual chronicles. Each volume attempts to emphasize an individual's contributions both in his or her own time and for posterity. For example, the voyages of Christopher Columbus opened the way to European colonization of the New World. Unquestionably, his encounter with the New World brought monumental changes to both Europe and the Americas in his day. Today, however, the broader impact of Columbus's voyages is being critically scrutinized. *Christopher Columbus,* as well as every biography in The Importance Of series, includes and evaluates the most recent scholarship available on each subject.

Each author includes a wide variety of primary and secondary source quotations to document and substantiate his or her work. All quotes are footnoted to show readers exactly how and where biographers derive their information, as well as provide stepping stones to further research. These quotations enliven the text by giving readers eyewitness views of the life and times of each individual covered in The Importance Of series.

Finally, each volume is enhanced by photographs, bibliographies, chronologies, and comprehensive indexes. For both the casual reader and the student engaged in research, The Importance Of biographies will be a fascinating adventure into the lives of people who have helped shape humanity's past, present, and will continue to shape its future.

Important Dates in the Life of Chief Joseph

Joseph is born in a cave near Joseph Creek in present-day Oregon.	**1840** **1847**	Henry and Eliza Spalding leave Lapwai; Joseph's formal education ends.
Joseph's father, Tuekakas, signs treaty forming reservation; Wallowa band becomes antiwhite.	**1855** **1863**	Attends council with Tuekakas who refuses to sign new treaty selling his land.
Tuekakas dies; Joseph becomes headman of Wallowa band; troubles begin with white settlers in the Wallowa Valley.	**1871** **1877**	General Howard gives Joseph thirty days to get his band to the Lapwai Reservation; Battle of White Bird Canyon; Battle of Clearwater; Battle of Big Hole; Raid on Howard's horses; Battle of Canyon Creek; Battle of Cow Island Crossing; Battle of Bear Paws; Joseph surrenders to Colonel Miles; Joseph arrives at Fort Leavenworth, Kansas; Joseph petitions Washington to be allowed to return home.
Joseph is moved to the Quapaw Reservation in Indian Territory.	**1878**	
Goes to Washington, D.C., twice to talk with President Rutherford B. Hayes; Joseph's view of war is published in *North American Review;* Joseph is moved to the Oakland Reservation in Indian Territory.	**1879**	
Twenty-nine Nez Percé are allowed to return to the Lapwai Reservation.	**1883** **1885**	Joseph is sent to Colville Reservation in Washington.
Refuses to accept allotment at Lapwai.	**1889** **1897**	Goes to Washington, D.C., to talk with President William McKinley and, on the same trip, visits New York.
Visits the Wallowa Valley for the first time since the beginning of the war.	**1899** **1900**	Visits the Wallowa Valley again.
	1903	Visits Washington, D.C., to talk to President Theodore Roosevelt.
Dies in his tepee at the Colville Reservation.	**1904**	

Chief Joseph

His name was Hin-mah-too-yah-lat-kekht, meaning "thunder traveling to loftier mountain heights." To his people, the Nez Percé, this was a strong name. It united him with the spirit of the tall, rugged mountains that protected his beloved Oregon homeland. Hin-mah-too-yah-lat-kekht became famous for trying to protect that homeland from white settlers who flooded in during the last half of the nineteenth century. Those intruders gave him the name by which he is best known, Chief Joseph.

Whites had already begun to arrive by the time Joseph was born in a cave near Joseph Creek in 1840. The United States was eager to see the nation grow, so settlers were encouraged to migrate west. The settlers were happy because this meant they would have the opportunity to own land that was fertile and full of natural resources. And the government was happy because this migration meant the new land could be defended more easily against foreign invasion. The only people who were not happy were the native Americans who already occupied the land. They saw the white settlers as foreign invaders. This invasion was the greatest crisis native Americans had ever known.

Joseph may never have risen to greatness if he had not been faced with this crisis. The coming of the whites threatened the very existence of his people and forced him to fight for their survival. Joseph was steeped in the traditions of his people, and from them he drew the strength, courage, and wisdom to carry on

In 1877, Chief Joseph became a tragic hero after his losing struggle against white encroachment on Nez Percé land.

In the nineteenth century, masses of white settlers migrated west to land already occupied by native Americans. When the Nez Percé fought to preserve their homeland in the Pacific Northwest, the result was the Nez Percé War of 1877.

his life-or-death struggle to protect and serve the Nez Percé.

Joseph was an intelligent, well-spoken man of peace. He did not want war with the whites, but he was determined to save his people and preserve their homeland. In June 1877, two young braves began the war Joseph never wanted, and circumstances forced him to abandon his homeland and join with other Nez Percé bands in a futile flight to Canada.

Pursued by the U.S. Army for more than three months, the Nez Percé fought their way to Montana, within forty miles of the Canadian border. There, so close to safety, their flight ended in surrender. Throughout the flight, Joseph served as the guardian of the people by protecting the women, children, and elderly and all their possessions. All this time, however,

the whites thought Joseph was leading the resistance and the flight. As a result, army reports and newspaper accounts of the war called him the head war chief and created a legend.

After the war and until his death in 1904, Joseph continued to fight for the well-being of his people and the return of his homeland. Because of his fame and his forceful personality, Joseph attracted attention to the plight of the Nez Percé and other native American tribes, all of whom had been forced onto reservations. Although he never got what he wanted most—to return to the Wallowa Valley in Oregon—the publicity brought improvements in the conditions on the reservations. It also made Joseph a symbol that future Nez Percé would embrace as a champion of their traditions and heritage.

Chapter 1

"I Will Tell You How the Indian Sees Things"

They called themselves the Nii-Mii-Poo, meaning the "real people." The name Nez Percé was given to them by French Canadian traders who saw some members of the tribe wearing long, narrow seashells through their pierced noses. The name Nez Percé means "pierced nose" in French. The name was accepted by the Americans and took on an American pronunciation (nez purse). Tribal

The Nez Percé homeland encompassed a twenty-seven-thousand-square-mile area, including parts of present day Idaho, Washington, and Oregon. Joseph's band lived in the lush Wallowa Valley in Oregon, pictured here.

members today, however, still call themselves the Nii-Mii-Poo.

The traditional Nez Percé homeland was a twenty-seven-thousand-square-mile area that now lies in north-central Idaho, the southeast corner of Washington, and the northeast corner of Oregon. By the early nineteenth century, the Nez Percé tribe numbered about five thousand people. These people were divided into perhaps 150 separate bands, each having an average of thirty-five people. Each band lived in a semipermanent village separated from the others by five to thirty miles. By tradition, the land around each village was for its use only.

A seminomadic tribe of hunters and gatherers, the Nez Percé met on the mountain slopes and prairies from April to September to dig edible roots, such as wild potato, biscuitroot, and camas lily. They then let these roots dry in the sun. Higher in the mountains, they picked and dried huckleberries in September. The men hunted for game, and that meat was also dried. During July, August, and September, the men caught huge supplies of the salmon that splashed up the many winding rivers. The fish, too, were dried or smoked. In the winter, the bands settled into their villages and lived off their supply of dried food.

Joseph's Band

Joseph's band, called the Wellamotkin, lived in Oregon's Wallowa Valley. Snug and beautiful below the Blue Mountains, the valley was lush with tall grass, roots, and berries. There was abundant wildlife. Here, the Wellamotkin lived somewhat isolated from most other Nez Percé bands, away from the main trails that crossed the homeland. In the nineteenth century, this isolation protected them from intruders for a while. The band was able to maintain its traditional life longer than some of the other Nez Percé bands.

Since the Nez Percé lived in separate bands, no single tribal chief governed everyone. The title of chief was an honorary one. It was given to any warrior who performed brave deeds, such as stealing horses from neighboring tribes. Chiefs played a number of temporary roles within their own bands. Whenever a specific event required a leader, the chiefs held a council and chose the chief with the most expertise in that area to take control. For instance, the best hunter would be chosen to lead a hunting party. The best and most popular warrior would be chosen to lead a war party.

Nez Percé Bands Run as Democracies

Usually, however, each band had one chief who could be called the headman. He was chosen for his wisdom, diplomacy, oratorical skills, spiritual powers, and physical strength. He settled disputes, acted as spokesman for the band, and ensured his

The Nii-Mii-Poo Creation Myth

Most native Americans have a legend that explains how their tribe originated. The Nez Percé legend involves Coyote, a mythical figure that appears in many native American stories. This version is taken from Mark H. Brown's book The Flight of The Nez Percé.

"There was once a monster which lived in the valley of the Clearwater River near Kamiah. This beast devoured all the animals that lived in the country for miles around and became such a menace that Coyote, that clever hero of many an Indian myth, decided it must be killed. Arming himself with a flint knife, he jumped down the animal's throat and stabbed it in the heart. Then he cut the body up into pieces and from them fashioned tribes of Indians which he sent to occupy the mountains and plains round about. Finally, he discovered that he did not have a tribe for the beautiful valley in which the monster lived so he squeezed a few drops of blood from the heart and from these made the Nez Percé."

A typical Nez Percé Indian village included a central lodge surrounded by tepees. The Nez Percé bands were democratic—all important issues were settled by general agreement in a council.

people's well-being. He set a good example by living according to the tribe's values of bravery, justice, honesty, generosity, and self-discipline. Although the headman was the most influential person in a band, he did not have the final say. All issues involving the band—deciding where to fish or when to wage war, for example—were decided by general agreement in a band council.

Even the council, however, did not have absolute authority to impose its decisions on individual members. Nez Percé society was very democratic and placed a high value on independence. Every individual had the right to do what he or she thought best. For instance, if a warrior had a good reason not to fight in a battle, he could leave and go home without damaging his reputation. But the chiefs did use their personal power, both physical and moral, to convince band members to obey their decisions, and most members did respect and obey the council.

Nez Percé Religious Beliefs

The Nez Percé believed that their personal and tribal power came from their religion. Each Nez Percé had a personal guardian spirit, a Wyakin, from which his or her name was derived. Wyakins protected individuals and guided their lives. Some Wyakins were considered stronger than others, and the stronger a person's Wyakin was, the more power and independence that person had.

One of the ways the Nez Percé showed their independence was by traveling widely. Individuals and small groups traveled as far west as the Pacific Ocean and as far east as the midwestern plains to trade with

A Poem for Chief Joseph

In 1983, Robert Penn Warren praised Chief Joseph's life in a lengthy poem called Chief Joseph of the Nez Percé *that includes stanzas about how Joseph acquired his Wyakin name in the traditional Nez Percé way.*

"I was born at the time of snow. My name—
It was Miats Ta-weet Tu-eka-kas,
The son of my father Tu-eka-kas.
But not my true name. Only after ten snows
Was I, a boy, ready to climb
Alone to the mountain, to lie with no motion
On the stone-bed I made, no food, no water, heart open
To vision. To float as in vision and see
At last, at last, my Guardian Spirit
Come to protect me and give forth my true name.
Three days I lay on the mountain, heart open.
All day stared into bright blue. All night
Into darkening air. Then vision, it came.
But by day, clear. An old man, he stood
And he gave me a name. I learned to say it.

I went down the mountain. My father I could not
Yet tell. But when the new-named ones, they danced,
Each dancing his new name, I danced. I leaped,
Skyward pointing, exclaiming, Hin-mah-too-yah-lat-kekht—
Thunder-Traveling-to-Loftier-Mountain-Heights. That
Was my name. That made my medicine true."

According to Wyakin tradition, when Joseph was ten years old, his Guardian Spirit gave him his true name—Hin-mah-too-yah-lat-kekht, meaning "thunder-traveling-to-loftier-mountain-heights."

Meriwether Lewis and William Clark hold a council with native Americans during their exploration of the West.

Lewis and Clark and the Nez Percé

Meriwether Lewis and William Clark went into Nez Percé territory as part of an effort to explore and map the West. President Thomas Jefferson had just purchased the Louisiana Territory from France and had commissioned Lewis and Clark to explore it for him. The purchase greatly expanded the United States. It included all the land from Canada to the Gulf of Mexico and from the Mississippi River in the east to the Rocky Mountains. Even though the United States did not own the land west of the Rocky Mountains, Jefferson also told Lewis and Clark to cross the Rockies into Oregon Country, which included the present-day states of Idaho, Oregon, and Washington. This is where the Nez Percé lived. Jefferson wanted to know if there was a navigable waterway from the Missouri River to the Pacific Ocean.

other tribes. Sometime in the early eighteenth century, they acquired their first horses in a trade with the Shoshone tribe to the south. Nez Percé legend says their horse herds are all descended from one white mare and her colt. By 1750, they had become expert horsemen and horse breeders, and every warrior had his own herd. From that time on, the breeding and trading of horses was their traditional source of wealth.

The horse changed the Nez Percé way of life. They were able to travel much farther, faster, and easier. Soon, it became a Nez Percé tradition to travel east to the "buffalo country," the Montana plains. There, they hunted buffalo with their friends, the Crows. These expeditions lasted for months, even years. Whole families and all their possessions went along. Because of these expeditions, the rocky, steep, narrow Lolo Trail over the Bitterroot Mountains to the plains became a well-worn route. In 1805, the members of the Lewis and Clark expedition came west over the Lolo Trail into Nez Percé country. They were the first U.S. citizens to visit the tribe.

In 1803, Thomas Jefferson purchased the Louisiana Territory from France. This acquisition more than doubled the size of the United States.

By September 1805, Lewis and Clark had reached the Rocky Mountains. Winter came early in the mountains that year, and food was scarce. Starving and exhausted, the members of the expedition sent Clark and six other men ahead to hunt for food. When they stumbled down the Lolo Trail onto the Wieppe Prairie on September 20, they found several bands of Nez Percé camped there to dig camas roots.

Clark's journal contains the first written account of the Nez Percé:

Proceeded on through a [beautiful] Countrey . . . to a Small Plain in which I found maney Indian lodges. . . . Soon after a man Came out to meet me with caution & Conducted me to a large Spacious Lodge . . . and great numbers of women gathered around me . . . and . . . gave us a Small piece of Buffalow meat, Some dried Salmon berries & roots . . . I gave them a [few] Small articles as [presents].[1]

The Nez Percé welcomed Clark and his men graciously. They were eager to meet whites because they wanted to trade with them directly. Trade with other tribes had brought the Nez Percé many desirable items, including guns, beads, ironware, cloth, and blankets. The Nez Percé knew

---

Clark's Description of the Nez Percé

In October 1805, after spending a little time with the Nez Percé, William Clark described these handsome people in his journal.

"The . . . Pierced nose Indians are Stout likely men, handsom women, and verry dressey in their way, the dress of the men are a White Buffalow robe or Elk Skin dressed with [beads] which are generally white, Sea Shells & the Mother of [pearl] hung to their hair & on a piece of otter skin about their necks, . . . feathers, and different Coloured Paints which they find in their Countrey Generally white, Green & light Blue. Some [few] wear] a Shirt of Dressed Skins and long [leggings] & [moccasins] Painted, which appears to be their winters dress, with . . . twisted grass about their Necks. The women dress in a Shirt of Ibex or Goat Skins which reach quite down to their [ankles] with a girdle, their heads are not ornemented, their Shirts are ornemented with quilled Brass, Small [pieces] of Brass Cut into different forms, [beads], Shells & curious bones etc. The men expose those parts which are generally kept from view by other nations but the women are more [particular] than any other nation which I have passed in *secreting the parts*."

these items came from white people, whom they called Allimah, meaning "people of the long knives."

The next day, September 21, Clark and his men traveled on to a small fishing village. Nez Percé folklore says it was in this village that the tribe's tradition of friendship with whites began. The friendship started because of a woman named Wet-khoo-weis, which means "returned home from a faraway place." Years before, she had been captured by another tribe in Montana and sold as a slave. Eventually, she was traded to a French Canadian who took her to Canada. She lived there among whites and was treated kindly, but after some years, she escaped and returned home to her band. Wet-khoo-weis told her people not to harm the whites because they had been good to her. She said they would be good friends if the Nez Percé treated them well.

Because of her words, the village headman, Chief Twisted Hair, helped Lewis and Clark complete their expedition to the West Coast by providing maps, guides, and canoes. In May 1806, Lewis and Clark again passed through Nez Percé country on their way home. This time, they rested there for about a month and met with a council of chiefs from a number of bands. Through interpreters and sign language, they told the chiefs that the United States was a powerful nation that wanted to build trading posts in Oregon Country. There, all tribes could trade for the white man's goods in peace.

Lewis wrote in his journal that the council confirmed the chiefs' friendship by promising "the whites might [count] on their attachment and their best services, for though poor, their hearts were good."[2] To the Nez Percé, this was a serious pledge.

Word spread throughout the tribe and was passed down through the generations: the chiefs had promised friendship to the Americans. This promise became a Nez Percé tradition that was kept, sometimes under difficult circumstances, until 1877.

By 1812, both British-Canadian and American fur companies had trading posts scattered throughout Oregon Country. The Nez Percé were not pleased with the results. The white traders who ran the posts tried to harass the Nez Percé into trapping beavers. The white men were willing to trade goods only for beaver skins, which were needed to make the beaver top hats then in fashion. The Nez Percé did not want to trap beavers or work for the whites. They wanted to trade horses and food for the whites' goods. When the traders refused, some braves resorted to stealing items from the trading posts. At least one Nez Percé was hanged for stealing. He was the first of many who would die at the hands of whites in the nineteenth century. As a result, the relationship between the traders and the tribe was strained.

The establishment of trading posts on Nez Percé land resulted in strained relations between white traders and tribal members.

Fur Trappers

By the late 1820s, however, the Nez Percé had become friendly with another group of whites, the independent, fun-loving American mountain men who came west to trap beavers. Through them, the Nez Percé were able to trade horses and food for the goods they wanted. Historian Alvin Josephy writes:

> The [veteran trappers] described the . . . Nez Percé in unprecedented terms. In many ways, they said, they were . . . honorable, sincere, and trustworthy. . . . In their letters and journals, the Americans commented on their manliness, pride, and dignified bearing, on their cleanliness, handsome garments, and combed and plaited hair, and on their arms and wealth in horses; and, because the Nez Percé . . . were the Americans' reliable allies against the Blackfeet [tribe], they spoke with appreciation of their courage and valor in battle.[3]

By 1830, this friendship and the guns and goods acquired from the whites had made the Nez Percé strong and wealthy. However, the chiefs could see the United States was far more powerful than their tribe, and they became interested in acquiring some of that power. Although no one knows exactly what the chiefs thought, Josephy and other historians think the Nez Percé apparently decided the whites' power

Two Nez Percé braves wear full war costume. One displays a combined tomahawk/pipe. According to historian Alvin Josephy, nineteenth-century trappers commented on the "manliness, pride, and dignified bearing, on their cleanliness, [and] handsome garments" of the Nez Percé braves.

came from special knowledge contained in the Bible, which they had seen the whites reading. So, in June 1831, the chiefs sent four braves—Black Eagle, Man of the Dawn, No Horns, and Rabbit Skin Leggings—to Saint Louis, Missouri, the nearest American city, with a party of mountain men.

No one knows exactly what the goal of this visit was. Historians think it is possible that the braves were sent to ask for teachers to come teach the tribe the Bible's secrets. The Nez Percé were very open to new ways and ideas. They may have intended to incorporate what they thought were power-giving ideas from the Bible into their religion. But, since the tribe had such strong faith in its own religion, it is highly unlikely they were asking to become Christians.

When the four braves met in Saint Louis with William Clark, who had become superintendent of Indian affairs, they had

George Catlin painted this picture of No Horns, and the picture below of Rabbit Skin Leggings, when they were returning from their trip to Saint Louis. No Horns died soon after this portrait was painted.

to make their request through interpreters. What the interpreters said gave Clark the mistaken impression that the Nez Percé wanted missionaries to come instruct them in the ways of Christianity. The news of this request spread to the East in 1833, and churches rushed to answer the call. But it was not until 1836 that the first missionaries arrived.

The First Whites Encounter Joseph's Band

Meanwhile, in 1834, Capt. Benjamin Bonneville, an army officer who spent years exploring the Oregon Country, became the first white to visit the Wellamotkin. He was greeted by the headman, Tuekakas, who

Rabbit Skin Leggings was one of four Nez Percé Indians who journeyed to Saint Louis with a group of mountain men in 1831.

was eager to meet an American. Tuekakas was Joseph's father. Writer Washington Irving, who later published a book about Bonneville's adventures, wrote that Bonneville was impressed by this meeting. Everyone in the village dressed "in all their finery" and stood in line to meet the visitors. "The chiefs then came forward . . . to offer the hand of good-fellowship; each filing off when he had shaken hands, to make way for his successor. Those in the next rank followed in the same order, and so on, until all had given the pledge of friendship. During all this time the chief [Tuekakas], according to custom, took his stand beside the guests."

After Bonneville's party was served a banquet of deer, elk, buffalo, fish, and roots, Irving wrote that "a long talk ensued.

Soldier-artist Gustavus Sohon sketched this drawing of the headman Tuekakas—or Old Joseph as he came to be known. This sketch is believed to be the only existing picture of Tuekakas.

The chief showed the same curiosity evinced by his tribe generally, to obtain information concerning the United States, of which they knew little but what they derived through their cousins, the Upper Nez Percé."[4] Upper Nez Percé was a term the whites used to designate the bands that lived in the northern part of the tribe's homeland. They called the bands in the southern portion, including Joseph's band, the Lower Nez Percé. Evidently, the whites thought there was a difference between the bands in these two areas, but, in fact, there was no difference. The Nez Percé themselves did not make this distinction. Later, however, the difference would become vast.

The First Missionaries

Following Bonneville's visit, Tuekakas became even more curious about the whites. In 1836, the first missionaries, Henry and Eliza Spalding, settled in the territory of the Upper Nez Percé near Lapwai Creek in present-day Idaho. Tuekakas began traveling to the mission regularly to talk with Henry Spalding, and he became very interested in the whites' religion. As a result, he was one of the first two Nez Percé chiefs to be baptized by Henry Spalding. According to Spalding's diaries, on November 17, 1839, Tuekakas, baptized Joseph, and his wife Khapkhaponimi, baptized Asenoth, were married and welcomed as members of the church. On April 12, 1840, Spalding baptized Tuekakas's new son, Ephraim. This son is believed to have been the future Chief Joseph. The name Ephraim seems to have disappeared quickly. One or two years

The Call Goes Out for Missionaries

Word about the four Nez Percé braves who had traveled to Saint Louis in 1831 was conveyed to the East in a letter from William Walker to G. P. Disosway in New York City. Disosway published Walker's letter, along with one of his own, in the March 1, 1833, Christian Advocate. *Disosway's letter was a call for action.*

"How deeply touching is the circumstance of the four natives traveling on foot 3,000 miles through thick forests and extensive prairies, sincere searchers after truth! The story had scarcely a parallel in history. . . . With what intense concern will men of God whose souls are fired with holy zeal for the salvation of their fellow beings, read their history! There are immense plains, mountains, and forests in those regions whence they came, the abodes of numerous savage tribes. But no apostle of Christ has yet had the courage to penetrate into their moral darkness. . . . May we not indulge the hope that the day is not far distant when the missionaries will penetrate into these wilds where the Sabbath bell has never yet tolled since the world began? . . . Let the Church awake from her slumbers and go forth in her strength to the salvation of these wandering sons of our native forests."

In 1836, Rev. Henry Spalding founded a mission near Lapwai Creek in Nez Percé country. Under Spalding's tutelage, the Nez Percé were encouraged to adopt Christian tenets and live like the whites.

later, another son named Ollokot (Frog) was born and baptized.

Tuekakas and his family, as well as many other Nez Perce, began spending months at a time at the mission. Because of this, they were greatly influenced by the Spaldings. As with all missionaries in the American West, it was the Spaldings' intention not only to convert the Nez Percé to Christianity but also to teach them to live like the whites. While the children attended school, the adults were encouraged to build permanent homes and become farmers. The Spaldings had begun to achieve some success when, in 1847, another missionary family nearby was killed by members of the Cayuse tribe and the churches closed all the missions.

Even though the Spaldings left, their influence remained. They caused a split in the Nez Percé tribe that is still not fully mended today. Many Upper Nez Percé

Eliza Spalding with her two young children. Although the Spaldings left Oregon Country in 1847, their influence irreparably divided the Nez Percé tribe.

bands near Lapwai settled down and became farmers. They obeyed the whites' laws and incorporated many elements of Christianity into their tribal religion. However, most of the Lower Nez Percé bands, including Tuekakas's Wellamotkin, did not adopt white ways. They resented the fact that the Upper Nez Percé bands were not maintaining the tribe's traditions. Furthermore, as more whites settled in Oregon Country, relations between the whites and the Lower Nez Percé deteriorated. These bands became increasingly antiwhite and followed their own beliefs and practices. Tuekakas, in particular, began to feel that the whites were greedy and untrustworthy.

A Break with Whites

In 1879, Chief Joseph tried to explain his father's change of heart toward the whites:

> At first our people made no complaint. They thought there was room enough for all to live in peace, and they were

MATTHEWNIM TAAISKT.

PRINTED AT THE PRESS OF THE
OREGON MISSION, UNDER
THE DIRECTION OF
THE AMERICAN
BOARD, C. F.
MISSIONS.
CLEAR WATER:
M. G. FOISY, Printer.

——

1845.

WANAHNA I.

TIMASH hiwash Jesus Christpkinih wiautsath kuph. Davidnim miahs awaka Jesus Christ, Abrahamnim miahs awaka David.

2 Abrahamnim miahs autsama Isaac; Isaacnim miahs autsama Jacob; Jacobnim mamaias autsama Judas wak askama;

3 Judasnim autsama mamaias Phares wah Zara, Tharmapkinih; Pharesnim miahs autsama Esrom; Esromnim miahs autsama Aram;

4 Aramnim miahs autsama Aminadab; Aminadabnim miahs autsama Naason; Naasonmiahs autsama Salmon;

5 Salmonm miahs autsama Booz Rachabkinih; Booznim miahs autsama Obed Ruthpkinih; Obednim miahs antsama Jesse;

6 Jessenim miahs autsama David, Miohat; Davidnim Miohatom miahs autsama Solomon, ka yoh awaka iwapna Urianm, kunimpkinih;

7 Solomon miahs autsama Roboam; Roboamnim miahs autsama Abia; Abianm miahs autsama Asa;

8 Asanm miahs autsama Josaphat; Josaphatom miahs autsama Joram; Joramnim miahs autsama Ozias;

9 Oziasnim miahs antsama Joatham; Joathamnim miahs autsama Achaz; Achaznim miahs autsama Ezekias;

10 Ezekiasnim miahs autsama Manases; Manasesnmi miahs autsama Amon; Amonnim miahs autsama Josias;

11 Josiasnim mamaias autsama Jechonias wak askamaka kaua Babylonpa panahnasankika immuna.

12 Ka kaua panahpaiksankika Babylonpa immuna, kaua Jekoniasnim miahs autsama Salathiel; Salathielm miahs autsama Zorobabel;

13 Zorobabelm miahs autsama Abiud; Abiudnim miahs autsama Azor;

14 Azornm miahs autsama Sadoc; Sadocnim miahs autsama Achim, Achimnim miahs autsama Eliud;

15 Eliudnim miahs autsama Eleazar, Eleazarnim miahs

Spalding translated the Book of Matthew into Nez Percé (above) in an attempt to Christianize tribal members. Although Old Joseph was one of the first converts, he became increasingly wary of white beliefs and practices.

learning many things from the white men that seemed to be good. But we soon found that the white men were growing rich very fast, and were greedy to possess everything the Indian had. My father was the first to see through the schemes of the white men, and he warned his tribe to be careful about trading with them. He had suspicion of men who seemed so anxious to make money. I was a boy then, but I remember well my father's caution. He had sharper eyes than the rest of our people.[5]

Joseph was only seven when the Spaldings left. Their influence on him was not lasting. Although he attended school for a short time and must have learned some English, he never spoke it in later years. He communicated with the whites through interpreters and sign language. After the age of seven, Joseph grew up in the traditional Nez Percé way, learning a chief's responsibilities from his father. But while he was roaming free in the Wallowa Valley, officials in the U.S. government were making decisions that would change Joseph's life forever.

2 "My Father Never Sold Our Land"

In the nineteenth century, the decisions of the U.S. government regarding native Americans were based on a policy called Manifest Destiny. According to this policy, the United States was destined to expand its territory over as much of North America as possible. The goal of this expansion was to increase the country's economic, political, and social influence in the world. Each time the United States acquired new territory, the federal government encouraged its citizens to settle there. Settlers helped to protect the new territory from invaders, and they increased the value of the land by developing farms and establishing towns.

The native Americans who already lived on the land were considered a hindrance to expansion because they caused problems for the settlers. Many of these problems stemmed from misunderstanding and intolerance on the part of the settlers. Whites, in general, considered their culture and religions superior to those of

A family poses by the covered wagon they used while traveling west to homestead land. The great influx of whites resulted in the relocation of native Americans to reservations.

As the United States expanded, the government encouraged its citizens to settle new territories. Reservations grew smaller to make room for whites, and many native Americans were increasingly disillusioned with the whites' land treaties and agreements.

the native Americans. They often treated tribal members like animals as they tried to rid the land of these primitive cultures and religions in the name of God and progress. When the tribes resisted, sometimes violently, the settlers reacted with shock and anger. Because native Americans were hunters and gatherers who did not settle down and develop the land, whites felt the tribes could not claim ownership of it. Therefore, they saw the resistance as the acts of brutal savages.

Settlers' Fear

As resistance to white encroachment increased, so did the settlers' fear of the native Americans. More and more often, they called on the government for army protection. The government quickly developed a solution to this problem. They used any means necessary to relocate all native Americans to reservations, land set aside by the government for an Indian tribe's exclusive use. Most reservations were established by a treaty between the govern-

ment and a tribe. But as soon as a reservation was established, new settlers appeared and demanded more land. The reservations continued to shrink as native Americans signed one treaty after another giving up more and more of their land. Even when new agreements were reached, the whites often did not keep their promises. They often broke these treaties by settling on tribal land. Native Americans became increasingly confused and angry as the United States grew.

The Louisiana Purchase in 1803 was only the beginning of the phase of westward expansion that would eventually bring white settlers onto Nez Percé land. In 1848, Oregon Country was declared a U.S. territory. The United States now owned the Nez Percé homeland. The future state of Washington was established as a separate territory in 1853, and Isaac Stevens was appointed its governor and superintendent of Indian affairs. He was also appointed to find a northwestern route for the first transcontinental railroad. These three positions gave Stevens the power to make treaties with all the northwestern tribes, including the Nez Percé. Through

In 1855, the U.S. government decided to settle land disputes in northwestern territories. Various tribes were summoned to a meeting in the Walla Walla Valley in Washington. A sketch by a government artist shows the flamboyant arrival of the Nez Percé.

these treaties, he planned to obtain land for white settlers and the railroad and also to confine the tribes to reservations.

Stevens was an arrogant, ambitious man who hoped to advance his political career by getting rid of the "Indian problem" in the northwestern territories. In 1855, Stevens and Joel Palmer, superintendent of Indian affairs in Oregon, invited the Nez Percé, Cayuse, Umatilla, Walla Walla, and Yakima tribes to a meeting in the Walla Walla Valley in Washington. Their goal was to persuade each tribe to sign a treaty establishing a reservation on part of their traditional homeland. Between five and six thousand native Americans attended the meeting, which lasted from May 29 to June 11.

A military observer at the meeting, Lt. Lawrence Kip, recorded the arrival of some twenty-five hundred Nez Percé, including Tuekakas.

> When about a mile distant they halted, and half a dozen chiefs rode forward and were introduced to Governor Stevens and General Palmer, in order of their rank. Then came the rest of the wild horsemen in single file, clashing their shields, singing and beating

their drums as they marched past us. Then they formed a circle and danced around us, while our little group stood there, the center of their wild evolutions. . . . After these performances, more than twenty of the chiefs went over to the tent of Governor Stevens, where they sat for some time, smoking the "pipe of peace," in token of good fellowship, and then returned to their camping ground.[6]

During the peace talks, Gov. Isaac Stevens held a feast for the visiting chiefs in the shade of an arbor. Stevens's ploys to win their favor failed; the chiefs resented and distrusted him.

Errors of Judgment

When his meeting with the Nez Percé began, Stevens made two mistakes that caused the negotiations to falter from the start. First, he appointed a Nez Percé chief called Lawyer as tribal chief to speak for all the Nez Percé bands. Chief Lawyer had been a particular friend of the Americans for years. Stevens did not realize that the Nez Percé would not recognize Lawyer as the tribal chief because each band was independent. Lawyer could not speak for the other chiefs.

Second, Stevens offended the proud, intelligent chiefs by talking to them as if they were children. Instead of being honest with them about his intentions, he told them about all the wonderful things the

Stevens designated one chief—who was called Lawyer for his persuasive oratory—to speak for all the Nez Percé bands. The independent bands of Nez Percé, however, did not recognize Lawyer as tribal leader.

government was going to do for them. For instance, he told them that the Great Father, the president of the United States,

John Q. Adams's Views of Native American Rights

In 1802, John Quincy Adams, who became president of the United States in 1825, defended the taking of native American homelands with the argument that their use of the land was not economical. As hunters and gatherers, they used too much land for too few people, Adams claimed. This quote is excerpted from Merrill Beal's book I Will Fight No More Forever.

"The Indian right of possession itself stands, with regard to the greatest part of the country, upon a questionable foundation. Their cultivated fields; their constructed habitations; a space of ample sufficiency for their subsistence, and whatever they had annexed to themselves by personal labor, was undoubtedly by the law of nature theirs. But what is the right of a huntsman to the forest of a thousand miles over which he accidently ranged in quest of prey? Shall the liberal bounties of Providence to the race of man be monopolized by one of ten thousand for whom they were created? Shall the exuberant bosom of the common mother, amply adequate to the nourishment of millions, be claimed exclusively by a few hundreds of her offspring?"

wanted to protect them from the whites. Native Americans already on reservations were happy, Stevens said, and he wanted the Nez Percé to have the same happiness. Then, he tried to hurry the negotiations so that the chiefs would not have time to think and resist.

The chiefs immediately knew that Stevens wanted to take their land for the whites, and they had heard that the tribes on reservations were not happy. The chiefs resented the way Stevens talked to them and felt insulted.

In the end, however, the chiefs all signed the 1855 treaty. They did so because the ten-thousand-square-mile Nez Percé reservation granted by the treaty included almost every chief's homeland. In return for giving up seventeen thousand square miles of land, they were to receive $260,000 in goods, services, and improvements to their land. In addition, the treaty stated that no whites were to be allowed on the reservation. The chiefs believed the agreement guaranteed their ownership of the land.

In the end, the chiefs signed the 1855 treaty. Gustavus Sohon's sketch depicts the chiefs participating in their first formal surrender of tribal lands.

Gold Seekers Encroach on Nez Percé Land

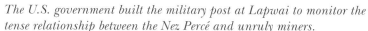

Tuekakas, angered by the way Stevens handled the negotiations and more antiwhite than ever, refused to accept any payment. He said he had given up nothing, so he was owed nothing. Life in the Wallowa Valley returned almost to normal. For the Upper Nez Percé, however, life changed drastically when gold was discovered on their part of the reservation in 1860. Before long, eighteen thousand miners were squatting on Nez Percé land. The situation was tense, with quarrels erupting over livestock, land, and water rights, but for the most part, the Nez Percé and the squatters remained at peace. The Nez Percé traded horses and food to the miners for gold, and they waited for the miners to leave when the gold ran out. Then, three Nez Percé were killed by drunken miners, according to the June 21, 1862, issue of the *Washington Statesman*. Although the chiefs demanded justice rather than seeking revenge, nothing was done.

Instead of kicking the unruly miners off the reservation, the U.S. government decided the best way to avoid future problems was to buy more land from the tribe for the settlers. The government believed that settlers, with their churches, stores, schools, and other signs of civilization, would have a stabilizing effect on the area. In 1862, the government built a military post, Fort Lapwai, on the reservation to watch over the situation and announced there would be another meeting with the tribes the following spring.

The council convened on May 25, 1863. Only Lawyer and the Upper Nez Percé chiefs were present. The government wanted all the Nez Percé to move onto a much smaller reservation than the one given to them only eight years before. The new reservation, which did not include the Wallowa Valley, would be centered around Lapwai, where Lawyer and the Upper Nez Percé lived. The government also wanted to divide the reservation up into twenty-acre lots, one per family, so the Nez Percé could become farmers "just like the whites." But the chiefs refused to

The U.S. government built the military post at Lapwai to monitor the tense relationship between the Nez Percé and unruly miners.

Nez Percé treaty negotiators pose for a picture at the 1863 council, where they were presented with a treaty that would further reduce their tribal land. This treaty permanently split the Nez Percé into two factions—those who would sign the treaty and those who would not.

sell their land, saying they considered the boundaries of the 1855 treaty fixed forever.

The council disbanded for six days, and when it reconvened on June 3, Tuekakas and several other Lower Nez Percé chiefs, including White Bird, had appeared. Joseph, now twenty-three, had come with Tuekakas. For two days, no agreement was reached in the council. Tuekakas and White Bird were so angry at the thought of losing their land that they refused to speak. On the night of June 4, the Nez Percé chiefs gathered in a lodge to hold their own private council. They argued all night about the treaty. By now, government promises of money and displays of sincerity had just about persuaded the Upper Nez Percé to sign the treaty, but the Lower Nez Percé were dead set against it.

A Final Break Between Bands

From outside the lodge, Oregon cavalryman Capt. George Currey listened in on the tribal debate with the aid of an interpreter. In his official report, he wrote:

The debate ran with dignified firmness and warmth until near morning when the [Lower Nez Percé] made a formal announcement of their determination to take no further part in the treaty, and then with a warm, and in an emotional manner, declared the Nez Percé nation dissolved; whereupon the [Lower Nez Percé] shook hands with the Lawyer men, telling them with a

Roosevelt's Views

In 1910, Theodore Roosevelt, who had recently retired from the presidency, explained in his book, The Winning of the West, *why he believed native Americans had no valid claim to their land.*

"Undoubtedly the [native Americans] have often suffered terrible injustice at our hands. A number of instances, such as . . . the whole treatment of Chief Joseph and his Nez Percés, might be mentioned, which are indelible blots on our fair fame; and yet, in describing our dealings with the red men as a whole, historians do us much less than justice.

It was wholly impossible to avoid conflicts with the weaker race, unless we were willing to see the American continent fall into the hands of some other strong power; and even had we adopted such a ludicrous policy, the Indians themselves would have made war upon us. It cannot be too often insisted that they did not own the land; or, at least, that their ownership was merely such as that claimed often by our own white hunters. . . . To recognize the Indian ownership of the limitless prairies and forests of this continent . . . necessarily implies a similar recognition of the claims of every white hunter, squatter, horse thief, or wandering cattleman."

Theodore Roosevelt insisted that the native Americans did not own the land they occupied. Rather, he compared their claims to "the claims of every white hunter, squatter, horse thief, or wandering cattleman."

kind but firm demeanor that they would be friends, but a distinct people. It did not appear from the tone of their . . . speeches, that either party was meditating a present outbreak. I withdrew . . . , having accomplished nothing but witnessing the extinguishment of the last council fires of the most powerful Indian nation on the sunset side of the Rocky Mountains.[7]

Neither Currey nor the Nez Percé told the government representatives of this split.

The Lower Nez Percé left for home that day. Before Tuekakas and Joseph left, it is said that Tuekakas tore up his copy of both the 1855 treaty and the Gospel of Matthew that Spalding had given him at his baptism. Tuekakas told Joseph, "When you go into council with the white man, always remember your country. Do not give it away. The white man will cheat you out of your home. I have taken no pay from the United States. I have never sold our land."[8]

Tuekakas retreated to the Wallowa Valley and marked his boundaries with ten-foot-high poles. "Inside is the home of my people," he said, "the white man may take the land outside."[9] He and the other Lower Nez Percé chiefs believed the matter was settled. No one else had the authority to sell their land, and it never occurred to them that anyone would. But that is just what happened.

Lawyer and the other Upper Nez Percé signed the 1863 treaty, which the Nez Percé call the "thief treaty." From then on, the Upper Nez Percé were called treaty Nez Percé or treaties; the Lower Nez Percé were called nontreaty Nez Percé or nontreaties. The government representatives, believing Lawyer had the authority to sign for the entire tribe, considered the

treaty valid. The treaty gave the Nez Percé $265,000 for 8,750 square miles of their homeland, including the Wallowa Valley. Their reservation was now reduced to a mere 1,250 square miles. The government expected all Nez Percé to move onto the new reservation as soon as the U.S. Senate approved the treaty and the land was divided into lots.

A Dirty Deal

Joseph explained later how the "thief treaty" appeared to the nontreaties:

> Suppose a white man should come to me and say, "Joseph, I like your horses, and I want to buy them." I say to him, "No, my horses suit me, I will not sell them." Then he goes to my neighbor, and says to him: "Joseph has some good horses. I want to buy them, but he refuses to sell." My neighbor answers, "Pay me the money, and I will sell you Joseph's horses." The white man returns to me, and says, "Joseph, I have bought your horses, and you must let me have them." If we sold our lands to the Government, this is the way they were bought.[10]

Because the United States was embroiled in the Civil War between the North and the South at the time, the Senate did not approve the treaty for four years. During those years, the Wellamotkin continued to live relatively undisturbed in the Wallowa Valley. The band knew, however, that difficult times were coming. Many white settlers had not waited for the Senate's

Between 1861 and 1865, white officials were enmeshed in the Civil War. Consequently, the Senate did not approve the 1863 treaty until 1867.

approval of the treaty. They had begun moving onto Nez Percé land as soon as the treaty was signed. It was only a matter of time before some of them reached the Wallowa Valley.

Anxious about these settlers, Tuekakas, Joseph, Ollokot, and many of the non-treaties joined a new cult called the Dreamer religion. This religion confirmed their traditional beliefs by proclaiming, for instance, "The Earth is our Mother; we must not wound her breast with ploughs and hoes." In other words, farming was for whites; the Dreamers remained hunters and gatherers. The cult was led by a shaman, or priest, called Smohalla, who claimed that some day soon all the native Americans who had ever lived would all be reborn together. There would be so many of them on their homelands that the whites would be forced to leave. Then, things would be as they had been before the whites came. Before long, however, the

unwillingness of some nontreaties to give up these and other religious beliefs would force them to abandon their homeland forever.

By 1867, when the Senate finally approved the 1863 treaty, Tuekakas was old, feeble, and almost blind. Joseph was assuming more and more of his father's duties. That year, whites came to the Wallowa Valley to survey it. Joseph watched them quietly and waited, but no white settlers appeared. For three more years, the Wellamotkin were left in peace.

The Death of Joseph's Father

Tuekakas died in 1871. As he lay dying, he said to Joseph:

> My son, . . . [y]ou are the chief of these people. They look to you to guide them. Always remember that your father never

sold his country. You must stop your ears whenever you are asked to sign a treaty selling your home. A few years more, and white men will be all around you. They have their eyes on this land. My son, never forget my dying words. This country holds your father's body. Never sell the bones of your father and your mother.[11]

Then, Joseph said, "I buried him in that beautiful valley of winding waters. I love that land more than all the rest of the world. A man who would not love his father's grave is worse than a wild animal."[12]

Chief Joseph was now thirty-one years old. He was married and had one daughter, and he was the headman of a band of about 250 people. From this time on, he dedicated himself to preserving the Wallowa Valley for his people. And because he knew war with the whites would destroy the Nez Percé, he was determined to use peaceful means. As a result, Joseph was outspoken about his people's rights, but he was diplomatic and willing to compromise in many ways. Many whites admired him and considered him fair and honest. Despite this, protecting his people and homeland was a difficult job from the beginning.

Early Conflicts with Whites

The year Tuekakas died, the first white cattlemen came into the Wallowa Valley. They had discovered the lush grass in the valley, which made perfect summer grazing for their cattle. Joseph and his brother Ollokot, who was a warrior leader, ignored them. But, in the summer of 1872, more whites came, and this time some of them began settling down.

After Old Joseph died, his policy of passive resistance was carried on by Joseph and his brother Ollokot, a warrior leader (pictured here).

Although Joseph was friendly with the settlers, the problems began immediately. The tribe's horses and cattle roamed free and sometimes broke down the settlers' fences to get into their gardens and fields. In turn, the settlers let their pigs run free and dig up the roots the band depended on for winter food. When Joseph complained to the settlers, they said they had a right to be there. When the settlers told Joseph he belonged on the reservation, he said, "My father never sold our land." As far as he was concerned, that was all he needed to say.

The Nez Percé traditions of truth and fairness were deeply ingrained in Joseph. Despite his father's warnings not to trust the whites, Joseph continued to believe that if the whites really understood the truth—that the Wallowa Valley had never been sold to them—they would go away and leave it alone. This was Joseph's major shortcoming in dealing with the settlers. He did not realize that the whites had no intention of ever going away. In fact, white settlers would come west in a never-ending stream, and they believed they had a right to settle all the land claimed by the United States. They did not want to share it with the native Americans.

Nevertheless, Joseph thought he would receive justice from the whites. For example, in August 1872, Joseph lodged a complaint with the Bureau of Indian Affairs, saying that the settlers and cattlemen should be forced to leave the Wallowa Valley. T. B. Odeneal, the Indian superintendent in Oregon, and John Monteith, the Indian agent at the Lapwai Reservation, were appointed to investigate. On August 23, they held a council in the Wallowa Valley with

In 1873, President Ulysses S. Grant ceded a 1,425-square-mile reservation in the Wallowa Valley to the Wellamotkin. Due to an error, the reservation was placed in the north, creating hostilities between the settlers and the bands.

about forty Nez Percé and perhaps thirty settlers. Joseph eloquently stated his case and convinced the two agents his people had a right to the valley.

Monteith wrote in his report of the meeting: "It is a great pity that the valley was ever opened for settlement. . . . If there is any way by which the Wallowa Valley could be kept for the Indians I would recommend that it be done."[13] Monteith ended by suggesting that the valley be divided between the whites and Joseph's band. Joseph's band was to keep the "upper," or mountainous, eastern part of the valley where their traditional hunting and gathering fields lay. The whites were to have the "lower," western part, where they had settled. Joseph accepted this compromise to keep his people on their land.

A Fatal Error

On June 16, 1873, President Ulysses S. Grant signed an executive order that gave the Wellamotkin a 1,425-square-mile reservation in the Wallowa Valley. But someone in Washington, D.C., misunderstood the recommendation, thinking that "upper" meant north and "lower" meant south. The order placed the reservation in the northern end of the valley, where all the settlers lived. The band was separated from its traditional supplies of food. The settlers were given the southern end of the valley, which was too high and cold to be farmed. Everyone was unhappy, and no attempt was made to correct the error. The quarrels between the settlers and the band, particularly the young braves, over range rights and the ownership of stray animals increased. The angry braves sometimes

Kennedy's Views

A message from President John F. Kennedy was used to introduce The American Heritage Book of Indians, *published in 1982.*

"American Indians defy any single description. . . . But collectively their history is our history and should be part of our shared and remembered heritage. Yet even their heroes are largely unknown to other Americans . . . except for such figures as Chief Joseph and his Nez Percé warriors of the 1870s. . . .

When we forget great contributors to our American history—when we neglect the heroic past of the American Indian—we thereby weaken our own heritage. We need to remember the contributions our forefathers found here and from which they borrowed liberally.

Before we can set out on the road to success, we have to know where we are going, and before we can know that we must determine where we have been in the past.

It seems a basic requirement to study the history of our Indian people. America has much to learn about the heritage of our American Indians. Only through this study can we as a nation do what must be done if our treatment of the American Indian is not to be marked down for all time as a national disgrace."

John F. Kennedy believed that we should not forget the rich history of the American Indian, commenting that "when we neglect the heroic past of the American Indian—we thereby weaken our own heritage."

threatened to use force to drive the settlers out of the valley.

Although Joseph succeeded in keeping the band under control, the settlers became frightened that the braves would attack. They sent word of their fears to the rest of Oregon. Then, their fear turned to hatred as resentment of the new reservation grew. They and many of Oregon's politicians began a letter and newspaper campaign to get Joseph's band out of the Wallowa Valley. Suddenly, Joseph, who had always tried to achieve peace through compromise, was being portrayed by Oregon's whites as a fearsome, untrustworthy villain.

Greatly concerned about the conflicts in the valley, Joseph traveled to Lapwai to talk with Monteith, but Monteith had changed his mind about the Wallowa Valley. He was angry because the whites blamed him for the creation of the reservation. He accused Joseph of causing the problems in the valley and told him he should move onto the Lapwai Reservation. Joseph, as a last resort, asked to be allowed to travel to Washington, D.C., to tell President Grant the truth. Monteith refused. Joseph returned to the Wallowa Valley and tried to keep his people out of sight of the whites.

By the spring of 1874, Joseph was both angry and confused. Not only had Monteith not moved the settlers off the Wallowa Reservation, but more were moving in. Joseph's young braves were getting harder to control. To make matters worse, braves from other nontreaty bands were talking to them about revenge for the murders and other wrongs committed by the whites over the years. Knowing that a war against the whites would be foolish, Joseph and Ollokot tried to calm the braves.

Looking Glass sits on horseback in an 1877 photograph. In the years preceding the War of 1877, Looking Glass—a nontreaty Nez Percé—vigorously opposed war with the whites.

Joseph said later:

Our young men were quick-tempered, and I have had great trouble in keeping them from doing rash things. I have carried a heavy load on my back ever since I was a boy. I learned then that we were but few, while the white men were many, and that we could not hold our own with them. We were like deer. They were like grizzly bears. We had a small country. Their country was large. We were contented to let things remain as the Great Spirit Chief made them. They were not; and would change the rivers and mountains if they did not suit them.[14]

The settlers were not forced to leave because U.S. Secretary of the Interior Columbus Delano did not want to antagonize Oregon's politicians and citizens. He was afraid of losing their support for President Grant and the Republican party in the 1874 election year. So, although he knew little about the problems in the Wallowa Valley, Delano ordered Commissioner of Indian Affairs Edwin Smith to reexamine the establishment of the Wallowa Reservation. Smith correctly assumed Delano wanted the entire Wallowa Valley returned to the whites, and the reexamination ended with this recommendation. Accordingly, in May 1874, Smith let Oregon's politicians know that he had decided not to establish a reservation in the Wallowa Valley. Even though President Grant's order was still in effect, Smith declared the whole valley open to white settlement. Since it was also exactly what the politicians in Washington wanted, Smith's violation of the order was ignored.

No one told Joseph about this decision, so the band could not understand why the settlers were allowed to stay on Nez Percé land. In fact, more whites were moving in. The band's anger at their presence continued to increase. Still, when Joseph, Ollokot, and other nontreaty Nez Percé chiefs, including White Bird, Looking Glass, and Toohoolhoolzote, met that year to discuss the possibility of war against the whites, they agreed to remain peaceful.

In the spring of 1875, Joseph may have heard a rumor that President Grant had changed his mind about the Wallowa Reservation because he requested a meeting with Gen. Oliver Otis Howard, the new military commander in the Northwest. Joseph asked Howard if there was a message for him from Washington. Howard said there was no message. Howard later wrote he sensed there was mutual respect and understanding when he and Joseph shook hands. "I think Joseph and I became then quite good friends,"[15] he concluded. Howard was to become Joseph's main enemy.

Wallowa Is Opened to Whites

The rumor was correct. On June 10, 1875, President Grant accepted Delano's recommendation and rescinded his executive order of 1873. The Wallowa Valley was now officially opened to white settlers. Monteith sent for Joseph and informed him of this decision. He also told Joseph that his band would have to move onto the Lapwai Reservation, even though it had still not been divided into lots. Joseph refused. Again and again, he met with the settlers in the Wallowa Valley, trying unsuccessfully to convince them his father had never sold their land. He also met with the other nontreaty chiefs who felt as angry and betrayed as he did. Now White Bird and Toohoolhoolzote wanted to fight, but Joseph, Ollokot, and Looking Glass still advised peace, fearing their people would be destroyed in a war against the whites. Although the final decision was for peace, many of the other chiefs began to feel Joseph's approach to the white problem was too weak.

Chapter

3 "My Heart Was Hurt"

All through the summer of 1875, despite Joseph's efforts, confrontations between the band and the settlers in the valley continued. The settlers began calling for troops to police the valley. Several times, the troops came, found the Nez Percé peaceful, and left. It seems some of those calls for help actually had nothing to do with fear of Joseph's band. Whites in the Wallowa area were deliberately calling for troops so they could profit by selling them food and goods at high prices. Partly because of this, some troop officers were more sympathetic to Joseph than they were to the whites.

Sympathetic to Joseph's plight, General Howard reported that it was "a great mistake to take from Joseph and his band of Nez Percé Indians that valley."

For example, in August, Monteith, concerned for the safety of both the settlers and the Nez Percé, asked General Howard to send some troops to keep the peace. Howard ordered troops led by Capt. Stephen Whipple into the valley. Whipple met with Joseph several times and was so impressed by him that he decided to investigate Joseph's claim to the Wallowa Valley. On August 28, Whipple wrote a report to Howard saying he thought Joseph had a right to the valley.

Whipple's report so impressed Howard that he included it in his 1875 annual report to the U.S. War Department. Howard added to the report: "I think it a great mistake to take from Joseph and his band of Nez Percés Indians that valley. The white people really do not want it. They wished to be bought out. . . . [P]ossibly Congress can be induced to let these really peaceable Indians have this poor valley for their own."[16]

An Act of Injustice Creates Further Misunderstanding

By the following summer, however, the government had still done nothing to resolve the situation. Tension between the settlers and the band was high, and it was

Some Whites Recognize Injustice

In 1868, the Taylor Commission, one of the groups appointed by the federal government to handle the "Indian problem," responded with a report that condemned the government's treatment of native Americans. By the 1870s, it was obvious the report had not made any difference.

"In making treaties it was enjoined on us to remove, if possible, the causes of complaint on part of the Indians. This would be no easy task. We have done the best we could under the circumstances. . . . We are aware that the masses of our people have felt kindly toward them, and the legislation of Congress had always been conceived in the best intentions, but it has been erroneous in fact or perverted in execution. Nobody pays any attention to Indian matters. This is a deplorable fact. . . . Naturally the Indian has many noble qualities. He is the very embodiment of courage. Indeed, at times he seems insensible of fear. If he is cruel and revengeful, it is because he is outlawed and his companion is the wild beast. Let civilized man be his companion, and the association warms into life virtues of the rarest worth. Civilization has driven him back from the home he loved; it has often tortured and killed him, but it never could make him a slave. As we have had so little respect for those we did enslave, to be consistent, this element of Indian character should challenge some admiration. . . . Surely the [government's] policy was not designed to perpetuate barbarism, but such has been its effect."

only a matter of time before violence erupted. It came on June 22, 1876. Two settlers, A. B. Findlay and Oren McNall, shot one of Joseph's friends named Wilhautyah. They wrongly assumed he had stolen five of Findlay's horses. Three days after the shooting, Findlay found his horses grazing near his home. The settlers were now near panic, afraid Joseph and his band would seek revenge.

Joseph was indeed very angry, but he went peacefully to Lapwai to talk with Monteith. Monteith promised the two white men would be brought to justice. However, a month later, Findlay and McNall had still not been arrested. On July 22, Joseph and Ollokot again went to Lapwai. This time, they met with Maj. Henry Clay Wood, a lawyer who was Howard's legal assistant. Joseph spoke to Wood about McNall, who, he said, was argumentative and aggressive. In fact, Joseph and his band were friendly with Findlay and blamed McNall for the killing.

In 1876, Chief Sitting Bull led the Sioux victory over Gen. George Custer at the Battle of Little Bighorn.

With great dignity, Joseph told Wood that

> since his brother's [friend] life had been taken in the Wallowa Valley, his body buried there, and the earth there had drunk up his blood, the valley was more sacred to him than ever before, and he would and did claim it now as recompense for the life taken; that he should hold it for himself and his people from this time forward forever, and that all the whites must be removed from the valley.[17]

Wood replied that Howard had asked the government to form a commission of five men to hold a council with Joseph and settle all the problems. He also told Joseph his case would be stronger if he avoided conflict with the settlers and allowed the American courts to take care of McNall and Findlay. Pleased about the coming council and sure it would grant him his land, Joseph agreed.

Unfortunately, by mid-1876, the consequences of a battle between another tribe and whites were affecting all native Americans. On June 25, 1876, the Sioux tribe, under Crazy Horse and Sitting Bull, had defeated Gen. George Custer at the Battle of Little Bighorn in Montana Territory. In this battle, Custer and his two hundred men were completely wiped out. News of this defeat frightened white settlers in the West so much that they demanded all

The handsome and ambitious Custer was no match for the Sioux. He and his entire troop perished in the fateful battle at Little Bighorn.

Custer and his men futilely shoot against advancing Sioux during Little Bighorn. News of the Sioux's stunning victory fueled fear and panic in settlers throughout the West.

tribes be put on reservations as soon as possible. Howard, in the meantime, had already made up his mind what the commission would tell Joseph. He had decided the only answer to the problem was to buy the Wallowa Valley from Joseph and relocate his band to the Lapwai Reservation.

Joseph, however, knew nothing of this, and he was determined to get justice for his friend's death. When McNall and Findlay had still not been arrested by September 1, Joseph formed a war party and challenged Findlay and McNall to come talk and settle the issue. They did not appear. After several days, Lt. Albert G. Forse arrived with troops to talk Joseph into disbanding the war party. Forse promised Joseph he would tell McNall and Findlay to surrender, and Joseph retreated peacefully. He had finally persuaded the whites to do something about Wilhautyah's murder, but he would not get the justice he sought.

On September 14, Findlay was finally arrested and charged with manslaughter.

McNall, who claimed self-defense, was not charged with anything. The Nez Percé, believing McNall was the murderer, did not testify against Findlay. Findlay was found innocent and freed. Joseph and his band apparently accepted this verdict, for they settled down in the Wallowa Valley to await Howard's commission. Joseph was sure it would end all the problems by giving the Wallowa band back their homeland.

Official Recommendations

The five-man commission, which included Howard and Wood, met with Joseph at Lapwai on November 13, 1876. The commissioners expected Joseph to sell his rights to the Wallowa Valley and move onto the reservation. They were very angry when he refused. Therefore, the commissioners recommended to the government that all the nontreaties be ordered onto the reservation "within a reasonable time." If they did not obey, force should be used to make them go.

When the government agreed to this recommendation, Monteith was appointed to enforce it. He interpreted "reasonable time" to mean that the nontreaty bands had to be on the reservation by April 1, 1877. When Joseph found out, he was sure it was a mistake. Howard and Wood had both agreed earlier he had a right to the Wallowa Valley, and he saw no reason for them to change their mind. So Joseph requested another meeting with Howard. Howard agreed to a meeting at Lapwai on May 3. Monteith's April 1 deadline was ignored.

The May meeting was the last chance the nontreaties would have to try to resolve the issue peacefully. The nontreaty chiefs met beforehand and chose the proud, fiery Toohoolhoolzote as their spokesman. Joseph described the council:

> Then one of my chiefs—Too-hool-hool-suit—rose . . . and said to General Howard: "The Great Spirit Chief made the world as it is, and as he wanted it, and he made a part of it for us to live upon. I do not see where you get authority to say that we shall not live where he placed us."
>
> General Howard lost his temper and said: "Shut up! I don't want to hear any more of such talk. The law says you shall go upon the reservation to live, and I want you to do so, but you persist in disobeying the [1863 treaty]. If you do not move, I will take the matter into my own hand, and make you suffer for your disobedience."
>
> Too-hool-hool-suit answered: "Who are you, that you ask us to talk, and then tell me I sha'n't talk? Are you the Great Spirit? Did you make the world? Did you

make the sun? Did you make the rivers to run for us to drink? Did you make the grass to grow? Did you make all these things, that you talk to us as though we were boys? If you did, then you have the right to talk as you do."
>
> General Howard replied, "You are an impudent fellow, and I will put you in the guard-house," and then ordered a soldier to arrest him.[18]

Joseph Agrees to Move

When Howard threw Toohoolhoolzote in the guardhouse, Joseph and the other nontreaty chiefs realized the final moment of decision had come. They had to either give up their land or fight. Since Joseph's primary concern was for the safety of his people, he agreed to move onto the reservation. For several days, the chiefs rode around the reservation picking out sites for their bands. Only after they had chosen sites did Howard agree to release Toohoolhoolzote. On May 14, Howard gave the bands only thirty days to move. Again, Joseph used his persuasive powers to help prevent Toohoolhoolzote and the young braves from starting a war.

Bitter and resentful, the bands prepared to obey Howard's command. It was a nearly impossible task. There was too little time to round up all their scattered livestock, so they had to leave much of it behind for the settlers to claim. Then, they had to move what livestock they had found, plus their people and all their possessions, across several flooding rivers. It took Joseph's people two days to cross the raging Snake River. Due to their knowledge and skill, they all made it safely, but they lost many

Howard's Version of the May 1877 Council

After Joseph's version of how Toohoolhool-zote had been thrown into the guardhouse was published in the North American Review, *General Howard wrote his own version for the same magazine.*

"Mr. Monteith explained: 'The law is, you must come to the reservation. The law is made in Washington; we don't make it.' Then, again, [Toohoolhoolzote talks about the chieftainship of the earth] and becomes fiercer and fiercer. The crowd of Indians are becoming excited, and I saw that I must act. . . . The record is 'The rough old fellow, in his most provoking tone, says something in a short sentence, looking fiercely at me. The interpreter quickly says: "He demands what person pretends to divide the land, and put me on it?" In the most decided voice I said: "I am the man; I stand here for the President, and there is no spirit, good or bad, that will hinder me. My orders are plain and will be executed. I hoped that the Indians had good sense enough to make me their friend, and not their enemy.'. . .

I saw that immediate trouble was at hand. Joseph, White Bird, and Looking-Glass endorsed and encouraged this malcontent. I . . . turned to [Toohoolhoolzote] and said, 'Then you do not propose to comply with the orders of the Government?'

After considerable more growling and impudence of manner, he answered with additional fierceness, 'The Indians may do what they like, but I am not going on the reservation.' After telling the Indians that this bad advice would be their ruin, I asked the chiefs to go with me to look at their land. 'The old man shall not go. I will leave him with Colonel Perry.' He says, 'Do you want to scare me with reference to my body?' I said, 'I will leave your body with Colonel Perry.' I then . . . gave him into the charge of Colonel Perry."

General Howard considered the Indians "disobedient" when they refused to be placed on reservations.

In their last days as a free people, the nontreaty bands had to ford the raging Snake River on their journey to their new home—a government-run reservation.

what you do! Playing brave you ride over my woman's hard-worked food! If you are so brave, why don't you go kill the white man who killed your father?"[19]

Wahlitits's father had been killed by a white man named Larry Ott in March 1875. As he lay dying, he made Wahlitits promise not to avenge his death. Wahlitits had obeyed his father, and now Heyoom Moxmox's words made him furious. "You will be sorry for your words," he said.[20]

By dawn the next day, Wahlitits had made up his mind to kill Ott, and he convinced Sarpsis Ilppilp to join him. They set off to Ott's house, but Ott was gone and did not return all day. The next morning, the two warriors, their hatred and anger fanned by the long wait, decided to hunt

of their horses, cattle, and possessions. On June 2, twelve days before the deadline, six hundred nontreaties camped together at a place called Tepahlewam near Tolo Lake. It was their last chance to gather as free people, and they decided to wait there together until the last minute.

Braves Resort to Violence

On June 12, with only two days of freedom left, the young braves celebrated their past war deeds with a parade. Among them were two braves from White Bird's band, Wahlitits (Shore Crossing) and his cousin, Sarpsis Ilppilp (Red Moccasin Tops), who were riding double on a horse at the rear of the parade. According to the Nez Percé oral tradition of the account, their horse stepped on some roots drying in front of the tepee belonging to Heyoom Moxmox (Yellow Grizzly Bear). Heyoom Moxmox yelled at Wahlitits: "See

Talk of revenge triggered violence in the band of White Bird (pictured). Two rebellious braves started a killing spree that ended in the death of between fourteen and twenty-two whites.

No Chief Wanted War

Yellow Wolf, Joseph's nephew, told L. V. McWhorter his version of the aftermath of the May 1877 council. This account was published in Harvey Chalmers's book The Last Stand of the Nez Percé.

"[Toohoolhoolzote] was kept in the guardhouse several suns, like a thief.

That was what brought war, the arrest of this chief and showing us the rifle!

Some young men talked secretly among themselves. To one another they said, 'General Howard has shown us the rifle. We answer "Yes." We will stir up a fight for him. We will start his war!'

The chiefs were not talking war. After the Lapwai council they gave orders, 'Everyone get ready to move to our new home. Round up horses and cattle, as many as can be found.'

That was done. Cattle were rounded up and herded south of Salmon River. Water was too high and swift for their crossing. All the young calves—there were many—would be drowned. So would the old cows. While this was being done the people assembled at Tepahlewam, our old camping grounds at Tolo Lake. There were about six hundred people in camp. Many old men, many women and children. The women dug camas which grew thick on the prairie, while men and boys had good times gambling and racing horses. I was with Chief Joseph. . . .

None of the chiefs wanted war. They held many councils to hear what the older warriors had to say. Some of these said, 'We will wait for those returning from buffalo hunting in Montana. Then will be decided what to do if war breaks.'

There were six leading chiefs. Joseph, [Ollokot], White Bird, [Toohoolhoolzote], Looking Glass, and Hahtalekin. . . . No chief talked or wanted war. . . . I am telling you about three times, no chief wanted war."

down and kill other white men who had mistreated members of the tribe. Before the day was over, they had killed four white men and wounded a fifth. Proud and exhilarated, the warriors rode back to camp to boast of what they had done.

The news spread through the excited camp. Some braves decided to join Wahlitits and Sarpsis Ilppilp in more killings the next day, but most of the people were confused and frightened. They began to pack, in preparation for hiding in a safe place, but the chiefs convinced them to wait. Joseph and Ollokot were not in camp. They had gone to butcher cattle and bring back meat, leaving Joseph's wife, who had just given birth to a second daughter, in camp. Joseph did not hear the news about the killings until the following day when a warrior named Two Moons rode out to tell him.

Joseph was horrified. Later, he said:

I would have given my own life if I could have undone the killing of white men by my people. I blame my young men and I blame the white men. . . . If General Howard had given me plenty of time to gather up my stock, and treated Too-hool-hool-suit as a man should be treated, there would have been no war.

My friends among white men have blamed me for the war. I am not to blame. When my young men began the killing, my heart was hurt. Although I did not justify them, I remembered all the insults I had endured, and my blood was on fire. Still I would have taken my people to the buffalo country without fighting, if possible.[21]

Joseph and Ollokot rushed back to camp and tried to persuade the bands to wait there until the troops arrived. They did not believe Howard would hold the bands responsible for the actions of two braves. But the braves of the other nontreaty bands would not listen. They had begun to think Joseph was a coward and maybe even a traitor. They urged the women, children, and elderly to find a safe hiding place. Sixteen warriors from White Bird's band and one from Joseph's band rode out to join Wahlitits in seeking revenge.

For the next two days, these braves rode through the countryside killing and looting. Before they were done, they had killed between fourteen and twenty-two whites, according to various accounts. Meanwhile, except for the Wallowa band, the rest of the nontreaties had retreated to a cave called Sapachesap on Cottonwood Creek. Joseph and his band had stayed at Tepahlewam. They were still hoping to negotiate a truce. But, on the night of June 14, white horsemen fired on their camp. As a bullet ripped into Joseph's tepee, he knew he had no choice but to join the other nontreaty bands.

Despite the actions of their braves, none of the nontreaty chiefs wanted war. They all decided to take their people to an even safer place, White Bird Canyon, and wait for the troops they knew Howard would send against them. Their hope was that an officer would contact them before attacking so they could explain what happened and avoid war. This was not to be.

The whites were in a panic. They did not understand the Nez Percé tradition that allowed individuals to act independently without their chiefs' approval. The whites were convinced that Joseph had deliberately declared war on them, and Howard agreed. "In his mind," historian Alvin Josephy wrote, "Joseph had been the principal menace among the Nez Percés.

Angry and bitter, Nez Percé braves attack a group of settlers. A horrified Joseph later said, "I would have given my own life if I could have undone the killing of white men by my people."

The Wallowa band was the proudest, the most cohesive, and the most ably led, and the most demanding of all the off-reservation groups. And Joseph, as its chief and spokesman, must inevitably be the key to the behavior of all the nontreaties."[22]

When Capt. David Perry set off with ninety soldiers and eleven civilian volunteers to find Joseph, his orders from Howard were simply to protect the settlers.

He might have avoided bloodshed if he had tried to talk with the nontreaty chiefs, and he might have done that if the settlers, eager for revenge, had not convinced him the Nez Percé should be punished for what their braves had done. When the troops reached a ridge overlooking White Bird Canyon shortly after midnight on June 17, there was no longer anything Joseph could do to avoid war.

Chapter

4 "I Would Have Taken My People to Buffalo Country Without Fighting"

Shortly before 4:00 A.M. on June 17, 1877, Captain Perry began moving his troops down into White Bird Canyon. The Nez Percé knew the troops were coming and had prepared to meet them. Yellow Wolf, one of Joseph's nephews, later told his story of the Nez Percé War to a white rancher and historian named L. V. McWhorter. Yellow Wolf said the Nez Percé warriors had spread around the ridge and canyon. They "all lay flat and watched" the troops advance, while a truce team of six braves under a white flag rode out to meet them.

If Perry had talked with the Nez Percé team at this time, the war might have been avoided. But no one knows if Perry ever actually saw the men approaching. He never mentioned it in his reports. The white man who did see the team was a volunteer named Arthur Chapman. Full of anger and hatred toward the Nez Percé because of the slaughtered whites, Chapman immediately fired his rifle twice at the approaching braves. Yellow Wolf said:

> The soldiers began shooting. That was how the battle started. . . .
> The three men with me now began shooting. A long distance! I, with only bow and arrows, could do nothing.

On June 17, 1877, Captain Perry deployed his troops down the rugged slope of White Bird Canyon. Unbeknownst to Perry, a team of Nez Percé braves waited to ride out and present a truce flag.

The soldier bugler rode close to the brink of that rounded cliff, north edge of the gorge.

Twelve other warriors joined us. One, an old man, Otstotpoo (Fire Body), made a good shot and killed the bugler. When the bugler fell from his horse, Chapman rode swiftly out from there. His soldiers went with him. We did not try to stop them.

We ran to our horses. Mounting, we rode at swift gallop . . . [to] higher,

Moments after the truce team approached the soldiers, one of Perry's men fired his rifle at the braves. The last attempt to avert war had failed.

Yellow Wolf, one of Joseph's nephews, later recalled how the Nez Percé engaged in a bitter struggle against the soldiers.

more level ground. . . . It was there the real battle was fought.[23]

The battle was quick and decisive. The Nez Percé charged the troops and scattered them into small groups. The soldiers were forced to flee for their lives. Joseph said later,

We numbered in that battle sixty men, and the soldiers a hundred. The fight lasted but a few minutes, when the soldiers retreated before us for twelve miles. They lost thirty-three killed, and had seven wounded. When an Indian fights, he only shoots to kill; but soldiers shoot at random. None of the soldiers were scalped. We do not believe in scalping, nor in killing wounded men.[24]

The battle at White Bird Canyon was quick and decisive. Although fewer in number, the Nez Percé force outflanked the better-equipped cavalry unit. While the spirited and purposeful braves held their ground, the soldiers were forced to retreat from the battlefield.

Uncertain Future

No Nez Percé had been killed, and only three were wounded. As the clear winners of the battle, they collected sixty-three badly needed rifles from the battlefield. Despite their victory, however, the chiefs did not know what to do next. The chance for a truce was gone, they had lost their homeland, and it was too late to go peacefully onto the reservation. It seems odd that instead of fleeing immediately, they stayed in White Bird Canyon for ten days. The most likely explanation for their behavior is that it took that long for the chiefs to agree what to do next. Each band was still an independent unit, so no one chief could take command.

The Mistakes That Caused the War

In his introduction to Chief Joseph's 1879 speech in the North American Review, *Bishop William Hare listed six "well-recognized principles in dealing with the red-man." By ignoring these principles, the whites caused the Nez Percé War.*

"1. The folly of any mode of treatment of the Indian which is not based upon a cordial and operative acknowledgment of his rights as our *fellow man.*

2. The danger of riding rough-shod over a people who are capable of high enthusiasm, who know and value their national rights, and are brave enough to defend them.

3. The liability to want of harmony between different departments and different officials of our complex Government, from which it results that, while many promises are made to the Indians, few of them are kept. . . .

4. The unwisdom, in most cases in dealing with Indians, of what may be termed *military short-cuts,* instead of patient discussion, explanations, persuasion, and reasonable concessions.

5. The absence in an Indian tribe of any truly representative body competent to make a treaty which shall be binding upon all bands. The failure to recognize this fact has been the source of endless difficulties. . . .

6. Indian chiefs, however able and influential, are really without power, and for this reason, as well as others, the Indians, when by the march of events they are brought into intimate relations with the whites, should at the earliest practicable moment be given the support and protection of our Government and of our law; not *local* law, however, which is apt to be the result of *special* legislation, adopted solely in the interest of the stronger race."

While the nontreaty chiefs sat and debated their future, Howard mobilized troops. Newspapers, magazines, and army reports carried the story of the army's defeat to people across the nation. These accounts made the Nez Percé famous and began the process of turning Joseph into a legend. The legend was the exact opposite of the truth.

Media and army accounts claimed that Joseph had deliberately started the war. The truth was that Joseph had done everything in his power to avoid it. They said Joseph was head war chief of all the nontreaty Nez

Percé. The truth was that Joseph had no more influence in war councils than the other chiefs. In fact, he may have had less influence because the other chiefs thought he was too much of a pacifist. The historical accounts say Joseph was a brilliant strategist who led the Nez Percé to victory at White Bird Canyon. The truth is that the Nez Percé, including Joseph, had fought and won the battle at White Bird Canyon without any battle plan at all. They simply took advantage of the fact that Perry led his troops into a position where they could not defend themselves. It was Howard who said Joseph was a brilliant military strategist. He said it so that he, as the commanding general who was ultimately responsible for all his army's victories and defeats, would not look so foolish when the Nez Percé escaped.

Chief Looking Glass originally tried to stay out of the war. He and Red Owl, however, joined forces with the other nontreaties after the victory at White Bird Canyon. With the nontreaties now assembled together, they numbered about 750 people.

Attempting to Outsmart Howard

Although the Nez Percé had not planned the battle at White Bird Canyon, the next step they took was well planned. They crossed the raging Salmon River, knowing Howard and his troops would have much more difficulty getting across than they would. When Howard, with four hundred soldiers and one hundred civilian volunteers, finally managed to cross the Salmon on July 2, the Nez Percé had already retreated to Craig's Ferry twenty-five miles downstream. The Nez Percé quickly recrossed the river to the east side and headed to Camas Meadow, which was in the direction of the Lolo Trail. The trail would allow them to escape to Montana if that is what they decided to do. Since Howard and his troops did not reach Craig's Ferry until July 5, the Nez Percé now had a good head start.

The nontreaties had also gained reinforcements—forty warriors from two other nontreaty bands, those of Chief Looking Glass and Chief Red Owl. The whites considered Looking Glass and Red Owl to be troublemakers because they had opposed the 1863 treaty, but they and their bands lived peacefully on the Lapwai Reservation and had not joined the war. On June 29, Howard had received a false report that Looking Glass was sending reinforcements to Joseph and planned to join him.

Without investigating the report, Howard sent Captain Whipple and two companies of cavalry to arrest the chief to keep him out of the war. On the way there, Whipple picked up some civilian volunteers. The troops and volunteers arrived at Looking Glass's village early in the morning on

July 1 and demanded to speak with him. The chief sent a member of the band, Peopeo Tholekt, to tell Whipple that the band was not involved in the war and wanted to be left alone. For some unexplained reason, while Whipple and Peopeo Tholekt were talking, Dutch Holmes, a volunteer, shot a brave named Red Heart in the thigh. The troops and other volunteers began to shoot, killing and wounding several members of the band. When the rest of the band fled, the volunteers looted and destroyed the deserted village. They rode away with many Nez Percé horses without arresting Looking Glass. Angry and frightened, Looking Glass decided to join forces with the other nontreaties, and Red Owl joined him. Although figures vary, it seems likely the nontreaties now numbered about 750 people—550 women, children, and old men and 200 warriors.

When these Nez Percé left Camas Meadow on July 5 and headed northeast toward the Clearwater River, Howard was still trying to recross the Salmon River. He then had difficulty organizing his 440 soldiers, 100 civilian scouts, workers, and volunteers, and all the necessary supplies and equipment. Therefore, it was not until July 11 that he caught up with the nontreaties at their camp beneath the bluffs of the Clearwater. Because Howard approached from a direction the nontreaties had not expected, he caught them by surprise.

When Howard's troops began firing on the camp, the Nez Percé quickly dispersed. Hiding behind rocks and trees, the warriors fought back. The battle continued all day, with no clear winner, but the badly outnumbered warriors could see they had little chance of victory. That night, when darkness forced a break in the battle, a number of warriors deserted.

The next morning, there simply were not enough warriors left to hold out against Howard's forces. "For a few minutes," Howard stated, "there was stubborn resistance at Joseph's barricades; then his whole line gave way. Immediately the pursuit was taken up by the whole force, infantry and artillery . . . and cavalry as soon as they could saddle and mount. The movement was decisive. The Indians were completely routed." [25]

Joseph Saves the Band

Shortly before the Nez Percé line gave way, Joseph had seen what was coming. Since his primary job during the war was as *mioxcut,* the chief responsible for protecting the nonfighting people and all their possessions, he rushed back to camp to help everyone escape. Although he got there in time to get the people safely across the Clearwater River, he did not have time to save most of their possessions. When Howard entered the village, his volunteers found large numbers of blankets, robes, food supplies, cooking utensils, and family treasures to steal and burn. In the meantime, Joseph had moved the people downstream where, at dusk, they camped near the settlement of Kamiah within sight of the Lapwai Reservation.

If Howard had chosen to pursue and attack the retreating Nez Percé at this point, he would probably have ended the war. Instead, he ordered his troops to camp near the deserted Nez Percé village, while he issued reports of his "important victory." Thirteen of his men had been killed and twenty-seven wounded, but he

Nez Percé retreat across the Clearwater River as Howard's troops fire on their camp. Although the Nez Percé lost only four braves in the fighting, the Battle of the Clearwater was a turning point. The Nez Percé were left with few supplies and an uncertain future.

had driven the Nez Percé from the field. In the process, he claimed, twenty-three warriors had been killed, about forty wounded, and about forty captured.

The Nez Percé later denied this claim. They insisted they had only four warriors dead, only six wounded, and none captured. They also insisted they had not been defeated. Yellow Wolf said:

> We were not whipped! We held all soldiers off the first day and, having better rifle pits, we could still have held them back. Not until the last of us leaped away did soldiers make their charge. Some tepees, robes, clothing, and food were left. The women, not knowing the warriors were disagreeing,

quitting the fight, had no time to pack the camp. Chief Joseph did not reach them soon enough.

> But we were not whipped! Had we been whipped, we could not have escaped from there with our lives.[26]

Still, it was a bad defeat for the Nez Percé. They had lost most of their supplies and several warriors. Worst of all, they were still fighting among themselves about whether they should continue to flee, stand and fight, or surrender. The argument was still raging the next day, July 13, when they decided to take the people across to the east side of the river again. There, they camped on a hill out of firing range. Howard followed them and established his camp opposite theirs on the west side of the river. Again, he postponed his attack. Although the reason is not clear, it is possible he was expecting the Nez Percé to surrender.

The Nez Percé had certainly given Howard opportunity to attack. It is obvious they were in no hurry to get away. By this time, they had discovered it was fairly easy to stay ahead of Howard and his troops. In fact, they had begun to call Howard "General Day After Tomorrow" because he always seemed to let them stay two days ahead. Yellow Wolf claimed the Nez Percé waited beside the Clearwater "into the third sun for General Howard to cross and give us war. He would not cross."[27]

When they saw Howard was not going to attack, the Nez Percé broke camp on July 14 and headed over the mountain to Weippe Prairie. Instead of following, Howard stayed at Kamiah for two weeks, doing paperwork, making plans, and waiting for reinforcements. In doing so, he lost his final chance to end the war quickly.

A Woman Joins the War

In December 1901, a ninety-year-old Nez Percé woman named So-ko-mop-o, whom the whites called Jean, described her participation in the war to Henry M. Steele, who taught farming on the Colville Reservation. This excerpt is taken from M. Gidley's book With One Sky Above Us.

"When Joseph and our people concluded to fight for his forefather's birthright, I was anxious to join him, but my husband protested against my engaging in hostilities against the whites. Regardless of his entreaties and objections, I joined Allocott and Joseph and went all through the campaign. I left my home and my husband to assist in the struggle, caused by the encroachment of the whites. To go into details of this long and bitter fight would take much time and resurrect many unpleasant memories. During Joseph's march I often wept in sorrow and shed bitter tears in witnessing the wanton murder of so many of my relations and friends. We often hid in the underbrush and willows to screen ourselves from the musketry of the white soldiers. After such engagements the men would come and tell us who had been slain in battle. Sometimes they would bring in the mangled form of one of our braves whose life was slowly ebbing away. We always cared for the wounded as best we could until death claimed its victim. We generally buried the bodies among the rocks and in secret places. We did this so the soldiers would not know how many had been killed."

Looking Glass was chosen to lead the nontreaties east toward the Great Plains, where they could form an alliance with the Crows.

A Plan Emerges

At Weippe on the evening of July 15, the chiefs held a council and, at last, made a decision. Looking Glass and Toohoolhoolzote argued persuasively that they should go stay with their friends, the Crows, in buffalo country. If the Nez Percé behaved themselves, they said, they would be accepted by the whites in Montana. And if there was trouble, they could join Sitting Bull and his Sioux who had escaped to exile in Canada.

Joseph and Ollokot did not like this plan. It would take them too far from their Wallowa home and force their people to live among strangers. They wanted to stay and try to negotiate with Howard. And if that failed, they were prepared to fight. But Looking Glass was so sure his plan would work that the council finally agreed with him and put him in charge of leading all the nontreaty bands to Montana.

This gave Looking Glass the authority to direct their activities and choose the speed and direction in which they traveled. In a sense, this made him the head war chief, which is what many whites call him, because he was in charge of the flight during much of the war. But the chiefs did not select him to lead them into war. They selected him to help them escape war. Reluctantly, Joseph agreed to accept Looking Glass as their leader, while he retained his position as guardian of the people.

An engraving depicts Howard's troops in pursuit of the Nez Percé. Because Howard always seemed to be about two days behind the Nez Percé, he earned the nickname "General Day After Tomorrow."

Monument at White Bird Canyon

In this excerpt from The Flight of the Nez Percé, Mark Brown explains that the monument on the site of the Battle of White Bird Canyon commemorates the death of the white soldiers but does not mention the Nez Percé.

"The burial of the thirty-four soldiers [killed at White Bird Canyon] was not attended to until June 27, ten days after the battle. Each was interred where he fell, and the burial ground is far-flung. In 1927, the remains of an unknown soldier were inadvertently uncovered by road builders. Early in September of that year a group of Idaho County citizens established near the site a monument, upon which appears this inscription:

Before you to the westward lies the historic White Bird battle ground of the Nez Percé Indian War in which 34 men gave their lives in service for their country June 17, 1877. Beneath this shaft lies one of these men who rests where he fell."

The Nez Percé decided to go to Montana because they thought the war was local. They thought that when they crossed over the border into Montana, the war would be over. They did not realize the United States considered the war with the Nez Percé a national crisis that had nothing to do with state boundaries. As long as they were in the United States, they would be pursued by troops.

That night, the chiefs rode around camp, telling the people of their decision.

They told the Nez Percé that they must not kill any white men or steal anything in Montana because they were leaving the war behind them in Idaho. Early in the morning of July 16, the 750 people of the nontreaty Nez Percé began driving their herd of more than two thousand horses up the wooded foothills of the Bitterroot Mountains. They were headed toward the Lolo Trail and toward one of the longest, most difficult flights in military history.

Chapter

5 "We Understood There Was to Be No More War"

When the settlers in Montana learned the Nez Percé were headed their way, they thought they were being invaded and became frightened. General Howard was still sitting in Kamiah. It was obvious he would not stop the nontreaties from crossing the Lolo Trail. Therefore, Capt. Charles Rawn and thirty-five soldiers from a new military post in Missoula, Montana, rushed to the Bitterroot Valley at the eastern end of the Lolo. Rawn's orders from his superiors were to stop the Nez Percé from entering the valley. On July 25, with the help of about two hundred civilian volunteers and twenty members of the Flathead tribe, his troops began building a log barricade across the Lolo Trail in a narrow portion of Lolo Canyon.

The Nez Percé, camped only a few miles above Rawn's barricade, soon learned what was happening. They were certain the people of Montana would talk peacefully with them, and so Looking Glass, White Bird, and Joseph rode down to the barricade with a white flag.

The soldiers, Joseph later said,

demanded our surrender. We refused. They said, 'You can not get by us.' We answered, 'We are going by you without fighting if you will let us, but we are going by you anyhow.' We then made a treaty with these soldiers. We agreed not to molest any one, and they agreed that we might pass through the Bitter Root country in peace. We bought

At the end of July, the nontreaties started up the arduous Lolo Trail, pictured here. When they reached the Bitterroot Valley at the eastern end of the trail, they found a barricade manned by Capt. Charles Rawn.

On July 28, the Nez Percé bypassed Rawn's barricade, which was soon dubbed "Fort Fizzle."

provisions and traded stock with white men there.[28]

Although Joseph and the other non-treaties, as well as the Bitterroot Valley settlers, evidently thought Rawn had made a treaty with Looking Glass, there is no evidence he did. Because everyone believed there was a treaty, however, the Nez Percé were allowed to pursue their route through the valley peacefully.

A Long and Difficult Route

The route Looking Glass had chosen to take to buffalo country was actually the longest and most difficult of all the possible trails. He had decided to go south through the Bitterroot Valley, swing east through Yellowstone National Park, and then north into the southeastern corner of buffalo country where the Crows lived. He chose this route because, except when it passed through the Bitterroot Valley, it kept the nontreaties away from white settlers and other, hostile tribes.

If they had gone either directly east or north, they might have escaped to Canada in time. However, Looking Glass was more interested in hunting buffalo with his friends, the Crows. And all the chiefs thought they were safe now that they were in Montana. As Joseph explained later, "We understood that there was to be no more war. We intended to go peaceably to the buffalo country, and leave the question of returning to our country to be settled afterward."[29]

For a time, nothing happened to convince them otherwise. On July 28, when the Nez Percé rode around Rawn's barricade, which came to be known as Fort Fizzle, Howard and his troops were still sitting in Kamiah. They did not leave until July 30. When they finally arrived at Fort Fizzle on August 8, the Nez Percé were camped at Big Hole Basin, one hundred miles to the south. Thinking they had nothing to

Unbeknownst to Looking Glass, Col. John Gibbon was in close pursuit of the fleeing nontreaties. He caught up with them on August 8. On August 9, Gibbon and his men charged the Nez Percé camp, catching the Indians fast asleep.

Rawn's Report on Fort Fizzle

The whites' version of what happened at Fort Fizzle was given by Captain Rawn in his official report of the incident.

"My intentions were . . . to compel the Indians to surrender their guns and ammunition and to dispute their passage by force of arms into the Bitter Root Valley. On the 27th of July, I had a talk with Chiefs Joseph, White Bird, and Looking Glass, who proposed, if allowed to pass unmolested, to march peaceably through the Bitter Root Valley, but I refused to allow them to pass unless they complied with my stipulations as to the surrender of their arms.

For the purpose of gaining time for General Howard's forces to get up, and for General Gibbon to arrive from Shaw, I appointed a meeting for the 28th, with Looking Glass. . . . The meeting was held accordingly, but I submitted to him the same conditions as before. . . . Looking Glass said he would talk to his people and would tell me what they said. . . . Nothing satisfactory having resulted from the conference I returned to the breastworks expecting to be attacked. In the meantime . . . the volunteers . . . who represented Bitter Root Valley hearing that the Nez Percés promised to pass peaceably . . . left. . . . On the 28th the Indians moved from the [canyon] to the hills, ascending the sides one-half miles in my front, passed my flank, and went into the Bitter Root Valley. As soon as I found they were passing around me, . . . I abandoned the breastworks, . . . and advanced in the direction Indians had gone. They did not accept a fight but retreated again into Bitter Root. At the mouth of Lo Lo and before reaching it all the volunteers had left me, . . . and I was obliged to return to this post [Fort Missoula]."

fear from Howard, the Nez Percé were prepared to rest there for several days.

This was one of the chiefs' biggest mistakes. If they had traveled quickly and kept going, they might have escaped. But they failed to realize Howard could send troops against them in Montana. And Looking Glass compounded the mistake by not posting guards at night or sending scouts back down the trail to see if anyone was following. Someone was. Col. John Gibbon, commanding 167 soldiers and a group of volunteers, had set out from Fort Shaw, Montana, on July 28 to follow and capture the fleeing nontreaties.

The Battle of Big Hole

At 11:00 P.M. on August 8, Gibbon and his troops stopped to rest just six miles from Big Hole, where the Nez Percé were camped. Gibbon's plan was to have his troops approach the camp under cover of darkness and attack the sleeping nontreaties at dawn. He was determined to punish and capture them.

By about 4:00 A.M. on August 9, the soldiers had crept within two hundred yards of the village. Suddenly, an old, half-blind Nez Percé man named Natalekin came out of his tepee. He mounted his horse and rode directly toward them. As he peered ahead into the dim light, trying to find his horses, he was shot down by four volunteers. Then, the soldiers and volunteers ran toward the village, shooting at the

Dazed and confused, the Nez Percé are showered with bullets as they emerge from their tepees. Women, children, and unarmed warriors were killed in the first attack. Soon, however, the Nez Percé rallied their forces and counterattacked. They fought ferociously until Gibbon's troops retreated at 8:00 A.M.

(Bottom) The site of the bloody and hard-fought Battle of Big Hole. Here, the Nez Percé lost fifty women and children and thirty warriors. Joseph later said, "The Nez Percé never make war on women and children; we could have killed a great many women and children while the war lasted, but we would feel ashamed to do so cowardly an act." (Top) The rifle pits dug by Gibbon's troops.

tepees. Caught by surprise in their sleep, the Nez Percé panicked and ran for cover in every direction. Then, after a quick recovery, they began to fight back fiercely.

After the Battle of Big Hole, Colonel Gibbon reported:

> The Indians being terribly punished in the first attack. Large numbers being killed in their lodges, etc. The Indians who escaped, however, soon rallied, and as our line was insufficient to cover the whole front of the camp, the Indians were able to pass around our flanks and take position in the willows and wooded hills in our rear, from which points they kept up a destructive fire on our men, who were exposed in the field. Every possible effort was made to clear the willows along the river banks of Indians. But as fast as they were driven out in front, others would appear in the rear.[30]

Many Nez Percé were killed early in the battle, including Wahlitits and Sarpsis Ilppilp, who had begun the war. Joseph and Ollokot, whose wives were killed, fought ferociously. Then Joseph, barefoot and wearing only a shirt and blanket, rounded up the horses and led them away from the soldiers. By 8:00 A.M., Gibbon saw he was losing the battle and ordered his troops to retreat to a wooded hill and dig in. They were immediately surrounded by warriors.

As soon as the soldiers left the village, Joseph drove the horses back to camp and took charge. "In the fight with General Gibbon we lost fifty women and children and thirty fighting men," Joseph said later. "We remained long enough to bury our dead. The Nez Percés never make war on women and children; we could have killed a great many women and children while the war lasted, but we would feel ashamed to do so cowardly an act."[31]

Long afterward, Gibbon wrote: "Few of us will soon forget the wail of mingled grief, rage, and horror which came from the camp four or five hundred yards from us when the Indians returned to it and recognized their slaughtered warriors, women, and children."[32]

The Nez Percé families quickly took down some tepees and packed as many of their possessions as they could. At noon, Joseph and White Bird led the people and horses south to safety, while thirty warriors, led by Ollokot, stayed behind to keep up the siege on the surrounded soldiers. Finally, at dawn on August 10, these warriors left to join their families in flight. Chief Hototo, better known as Lean Elk or Poker Joe, was now in charge of leading the flight. Looking Glass, having failed to lead his people to safety, was in disgrace.

The Battle of Big Hole has been described as one of the hardest-fought, bloodiest battles in the history of warfare. It attracted the attention of the nation and, indeed, of the world. Howard was the commanding general, so the public blamed him for what they considered a defeat, even though he had not been in the battle. In fact, Howard did not fight in any of

A drawing by Peo Peo Tholekt of the Battle of Big Hole. While there was no clear winner at Big Hole, both sides suffered many losses.

the battles. As Yellow Wolf said, "In all the war, General Howard never came where we could see him."[33]

Although the U.S. Army had fewer casualties—thirty-four dead and forty-four wounded—they had not captured the Nez Percé and ended the war. The Nez Percé had escaped, but they had lost many warriors. Their fighting power was greatly diminished.

A Plan of Survival

In fact, there was no clear winner. The most that can be said is that each side had learned something. Howard, who did not arrive at Big Hole until 9:00 A.M. on August 11, now knew he had greatly underestimated the strength and courage of the Nez Percé. The Nez Percé, on the other hand, knew their very survival was at stake in this war. They were now traveling as fast as they could and guarding carefully against surprise attacks. And now, all whites were considered enemies.

This new attitude explains what happened when the Nez Percé camped at Horse Prairie, southeast of Big Hole, on August 12. There, angry young warriors attacked white settlers, killing nine white men. They also stole horses and ransacked houses. At no time did they kill any women or children or mutilate any bodies. Although the chiefs could not control the warriors, it is unlikely that they took part in these raids.

The nontreaties headed south from Horse Prairie, through the Bannack Pass, and back into Idaho. They were hoping to throw Howard off their trail, but Howard had correctly anticipated their plan. He

was now in hot pursuit, planning to meet them near Camas Meadow. He caught up with them there on August 19 and stopped at Camp Callaway, fifteen miles from the Nez Percé village, under the watchful, hidden eyes of the Nez Percé scouts.

A Mistaken Capture Brings Good Fortune

That night, twenty-eight warriors, including Yellow Wolf and Ollokot, went into Camp Callaway and executed a daring raid. They hoped to capture Howard's horses so the cavalry could not follow them. Not until dawn did the warriors see that, instead of horses, they had actually captured a herd of two hundred mules. Yellow Wolf said:

> After traveling a little way, driving our captured horses, sun broke. We could begin to see our prize. Getting more light, we looked. Eeh! Nothing but mules—all mules! . . . I did not know, did not understand why the Indians could not know the mules. Why they did not get the cavalry horses. That was the object the chiefs had in mind—why the raid was made. . . .
>
> We stayed the rest of that sun and all night at the same camp. Not until next morning did we move to another place. Scouts watching General Howard, we kept moving every day. The soldiers did not hurry to follow us. They slowed after losing their pack mules.[34]

Only two warriors were slightly wounded in the raid, but one soldier was killed and seven were wounded. Furthermore, without his pack mules to carry the supplies his soldiers needed, Howard could not move rapidly in pursuit of the Nez Percé. U.S. citizens, who were closely following the course of the war, began to laugh at "General Day After Tomorrow" when they read things like this poem in the newspaper.

Our Volunteers

Lay low boys, it is a general attack
Down in the creek or you'll get shot in the back,
I pledge you my word I wish I hadn't come,
And I'll bet you ten to one we'll have to foot it home.
Oh, I am one of the volunteers,
Who marched right home on the tramp, tramp,
When Joseph set the boys afoot,
At the battle of Callaway's Camp.[35]

The Nez Percé had accomplished more than they intended with the raid on Camp Callaway. Although Howard did not realize it at the time, he had lost his chance to catch up with the nontreaties and stop them. His mobility was so severely hampered that he could not take advantage of the small, fifteen-mile distance between the two camps. The Nez Percé stayed on Camas Meadow all day on August 20 to gather food. Then, they hurried through the Targhee Pass into Yellowstone National Park.

Yellowstone, the country's first national park, was established in March 1872. When the Nez Percé entered it in August 1877, it was still total wilderness. No roads or facilities had yet been built. Nevertheless, more than five hundred adventurous tourists visited it each year. During their passage through the park, most of the Nez Percé moved forward peacefully and steadily. But a group of young warriors roamed far and wide throughout the park. Four times in their wanderings, they encountered campers.

Encounters with Campers

The first camper the warriors captured was an elderly prospector named Shively. They gave him a horse and asked him to help them scout out trails through the park. He traveled with the nontreaties for a week and was then released. When Shively was interviewed by the newspapers, he indicated that he was treated well and enjoyed himself.

The second incident happened on August 24. Several Nez Percé warriors entered a camp of eleven tourists. The warriors demanded coffee and bacon and threatened the campers. The campers decided to follow the warriors back to the Nez Percé camp to talk to the chiefs. The chiefs held a council and let them go. Half an hour down the trail, the campers were attacked by several warriors. Most of the campers escaped into the wilderness, but two men were wounded. Three people, Mrs. George Cowan and her brother and sister, Frank and Ida Carpenter, were recaptured and taken back to camp.

The captives spent the night by Joseph's camp fire and were then released unharmed. Mrs. Cowan later reported that most of the Nez Percé seemed happy and carefree but not Joseph.

> My brother tried to converse with Chief Joseph, but without avail. The Chief sat by the fire, sombre and silent, foreseeing in his gloomy meditations possibly the unhappy ending of his campaign. The 'noble red man' we read of was more nearly impersonated in this Indian than in any I ever met. Grave and dignified, he looked a chief.[36]

On another occasion, the warriors captured a man named Irwin. Irwin told them

Eyewitness Account of the Nez Percé in Yellowstone

When a prospector named Shively escaped from the Nez Percé after traveling with them in Yellowstone for a week, he gave the only known wartime account of the Nez Percé camp to a newspaper called the New Northwest. *It was published on September 14, 1877.*

"There are from 600 to 800 Nez Percés in the band. Of these 250 are warriors but all will fight that can carry a gun. They have almost 2,000 head of good average horses. Every lodge drives its own horses in front of it when traveling, each lodge keeping its band separate. The line is thus strung out so that they are three hours getting into camp. . . . They seemed at first anxious about the soldiers overtaking them but soon got over that, and had no intimation any troops were trying to intercept them in front. They kept no scouts ahead and after crossing the Yellowstone had no rear guard. . . .

So far as he could notice no particular chief seemed to be in command. All matters were decided in a council of several chiefs. White Bird was not known to him at all, as such, but thinks he was present in the councils in about a dozen of which Shively participated. Joseph is about 35 years of age, six feet high, and always in a pleasant mood, greeting him each time with a nod and smile. Looking Glass is 50 or 60 years old. He wears a white feather. Joseph wears one eagle feather. . . . They say they have lost 43 warriors altogether. . . . They had but 10 or 12 wounded with them and one was dying when Shively escaped. They said they would fight soldiers but did not want to fight citizens."

where another party of ten tourists was camped. After escaping on September 1, Irwin ran into Howard, who was slowly advancing in pursuit of the Nez Percé. He was able to give Howard valuable information about the nontreaties' circumstances and position.

Meanwhile, the warriors had gone looking for the other party of tourists. The ten men in this group saw the warriors approaching, and nine of them escaped, although two were wounded. The tenth was killed. These episodes were reported in the newspapers, and the people of Montana grew even more terrified. They could not know that most of the nontreaties did not approve of these attacks. Yellow Wolf called the warriors who participated "bad boys."

The wounded and hungry Nez Percé thread their way along steep and difficult trails leading to Canada— and safety.

Howard's Pursuit

As the nontreaties threaded their way through the park toward the Clark Fork of the Yellowstone River, they were followed closely by Howard's scouts, including fifty members of the Bannock tribe. Howard and his troops were taking an easier, more northerly route, planning to catch up with the Nez Percé at the Clark Fork. Ahead of the Nez Percé, Col. Samuel Sturgis and his troops had reached the mouth of the Clark Fork near Heart Mountain at the eastern end of the park. To the north and south, three more commands were guarding the other river valleys. The nontreaties were now surrounded by troops, and Howard was certain he would catch them this time.

Howard was wrong. While Sturgis was waiting for the Nez Percé to arrive at the mouth of the Clark Fork, he sent out three scouting details. The scouts told him they believed the Nez Percé had taken another

Newspaper Account of the War

"In view of the bad effect [a Nez Percé] success and escape would have on other Indians, and in view of the evil they would probably hereafter do Montana, this concentration of forces, and the determination to destroy them, is in the highest degree satisfying. We are largely indebted for it to the presence of General Sherman in Montana, who has had the lion in him roused by the defiant progress of the Nez Percés and by personal attention to the movement of troops has raised up an army on the four sides of Joseph just when it seemed most probably that he was about to escape, scot free, except for the blow Gibbon struck him, and laden with booty, into the great open country of the hostiles. We wait now hopefully for news that the Nez Percés have been struck hard and fatally. They are too brave and dangerous a foe to escape, for their escape unscathed means still darker days for the border."

route, and Sturgis moved his troops toward the Shoshone River. Well aware of the troops' movements, the nontreaties escaped over the Absaroka Mountains through the hole left by Sturgis's departure.

Howard's scout, S. G. Fisher, described this escape in his journal entry of September 10:

After leaving the summit the enemy followed the trail towards the [Shoshone River] about two miles, and then attempted to elude pursuit by concealing their trail. To do this, the hostiles "milled," drove their ponies around in every direction . . . [to hide their tracks, and] instead of going out of the basin in the direction they had been traveling and across an open plain, they turned short off to the north, passing along the steep side of the mountain through the timber [hidden out of sight] for several miles.[37]

When Howard and Sturgis finally met on September 11, the Nez Percé were already fifty miles ahead. Because Sturgis's horses were in better shape, Howard sent him in swift pursuit with four hundred cavalrymen.

When the nontreaties reached the Clark Fork, Looking Glass went on ahead to seek help from the Crows. But just like the Flatheads, the Crows refused to help. Evidently, they considered the war a lost cause. The nontreaties, who had expected help from these tribes, were left without a single ally. They would soon discover their friends, the Crows, had become their enemies.

Chapter

6 "I Will Fight No More Forever"

When the Nez Percé left Yellowstone National Park, they traveled north along the Clark Fork to the Yellowstone River Valley in Montana. This was the buffalo country where they had hoped to settle with the Crows. Now, they had no chance of settling here. To avoid a battle they could not hope to win, they had to keep moving. Their only hope for freedom was to escape to Canada, and they were moving with great speed toward that goal.

When Sturgis finally caught up with the nontreaties, he spotted them two miles away, moving toward the entrance to Canyon Creek. The cavalry galloped off in pursuit. The Nez Percé saw them and raced for the entrance. While the people ran for safety, warriors sniped at the soldiers from behind rocks on either side of the entrance to cover the retreat. All the nontreaties escaped.

Sturgis had three men killed and eleven wounded. He also lost forty-one horses. Only one Nez Percé died in this battle, and he was killed by either a Bannock or a Crow. Far from helping the Nez Percé, members of these tribes were taking advantage of their predicament. They were

Col. Samuel Sturgis caught up with the Nez Percé at Canyon Creek, pictured here. Nez Percé sharpshooters held off Sturgis and his men while the rest of the nontreaties ran for safety.

harassing the nontreaties from the rear as they fled, stealing horses and possessions. During the flight through Canyon Creek, the Crows stole forty Nez Percé horses.

By continuing to flee until well after dark, the nontreaties made it through Canyon Creek. In the next few days, they traveled the 150 miles to the Musselshell River at a rapid pace. Sturgis followed, but their pace was too fast for him, just as it had been for Howard. "I find it impossible for my command to gain upon them," his message to Howard read, "and their direction is taking me further and further from supplies. I have . . . reluctantly determined to abandon a hopeless pursuit before my horses are completely destroyed." [38]

Sturgis made camp at the Musselshell, where he was joined by Howard on September 20. The nontreaties continued to move rapidly north toward the Missouri River, but they were beginning to feel safer. It was obvious that neither Howard nor Sturgis would ever catch them. Now, it was the speed of their flight that seemed to pose the greatest danger. The people were tired. The elderly, the sick, and women giving birth could not keep up. Often, they were left behind at their own request. When the nontreaties reached the Cow Island crossing of the Missouri River on September 23, it is likely there were only about 650 people.

Joseph's Band Is Resupplied

In September, the Cow Island crossing was the most northerly point on the Missouri that was reachable by steamboat. Because of this, all the supplies for settlements and forts farther north in Montana were brought here and stored. The supplies were guarded by a dozen soldiers under Sgt. William Moelchert. They had heard the Nez Percé were coming and were prepared.

The nontreaties camped two miles from the crossing, and several warriors went to Cow Island to ask for supplies. Moelchert refused, even after the warriors offered to pay. Yellow Wolf recalled:

> [B]efore night came, we took food as wanted. Each family took maybe two sacks flour, one sack rice, one sack beans, plenty coffee, sugar, hardtack. Some took bacon. Everything to eat.
>
> All this we captured from the soldiers. We did not starve that sun, that night. Whoever wanted them, took pans, cooking pots, cups, buckets. Women all helped themselves. When everybody had what they wanted, some bad boys set fire to the remaining. It was a big fire!
>
> We warriors stayed there all night, watching and exchanging shots with the soldiers. The chiefs who made rulings were at camp. They said, "Let's quit! Soldiers are under bank. We can do nothing. Nobody killed and we have plenty of food."
>
> A man was sent who told us what the chiefs said. The older warriors got together and minded the order. We turned from those soldiers, ending the shooting. It had been nearly like play. [39]

Following this incident, a guard named Michael Foley sent the following message to his commanding officer: "Chief Joseph is here, and says he will surrender for two hundred bags of sugar. I told him to surrender without the sugar. He took the sugar and will not surrender. What will I do?" [40]

The next day, the Nez Percé headed north toward the Bear Paw Mountains. That night, the chiefs held a council and again put Looking Glass in charge of leading the escape. Lean Elk, who had done a good job keeping them safe, wanted to continue their rapid flight to Canada. Looking Glass said the people and horses were exhausted. Now that they were safe from Howard and Sturgis, he said, they could rest and go at a slower pace. Lean Elk replied, "All right, Looking Glass, you can lead. I am trying to save the people, doing my best to cross into Canada before the soldiers find us. You can take command, but I think we will be caught and killed."[41]

On September 18, the ambitious Nelson A. Miles joined the last ditch effort to catch Chief Joseph and his people.

Another Battle

Lean Elk was right. There was a new danger the Nez Percé did not know about: another command had entered the war. On September 18, Col. Nelson Miles had left Fort Keogh in Montana with 383 men to intercept the Nez Percé at the Bear Paw

Mountains. He was moving fast, and he was determined to advance his career by capturing Chief Joseph and his people.

For the next four days, the Nez Percé made short marches while the warriors hunted buffalo. At noon on September 29, when they reached Snake Creek near the Bear Paws, Looking Glass decided to stay and make camp for the night. They were only forty miles from the Canadian border.

Still pushing north toward Canada, the Nez Percé camped near the Bear Paw Mountains. Discovering their encampment, Nelson and his men opened fire.

Early the next morning, Miles discovered their camp and charged. "This was the fourth army, each of which outnumbered our fighting force, that we had encountered within sixty days," said Joseph later.

We had no knowledge of General Miles's army until a short time before he made a charge upon us, cutting our camp in two, and capturing nearly all of our horses. About seventy men, myself among them, were cut off. My little daughter, twelve years of age, was with me. I gave her a rope, and told her to catch a horse and join the others who were cut off from the camp. I have not seen her since, but I have learned that she is alive and well.

I thought of my wife and children, who were now surrounded by soldiers, and I resolved to go to them or die. With a prayer in my mouth to the Great Spirit Chief who rules above, I dashed unarmed through the line of soldiers. It seemed to me that there were guns on every side, before and behind me. My clothes were cut to pieces and my horse was wounded, but I was not hurt. As I reached the door of my lodge, my wife handed me my rifle, saying: "Here's your gun. Fight!"

The soldiers kept up a continuous fire. Six of my men were killed in one spot near me. Ten or twelve soldiers charged into our camp and got possession of two lodges, killing three Nez Percés and losing three of their men, who fell inside our lines. I called my men to drive them back. We fought at close range, not more than twenty steps apart, and drove the soldiers back upon their main line, leaving their dead in

The site of the Battle of Bear Paws, situated only forty miles from the Canadian border.

our hands. We secured their arms and ammunition. We lost, the first day and night, eighteen men and three women.[42]

Among the Nez Percé dead were some of their best warriors: Ollokot, Toohoolhoolzote, and Lean Elk. But they had kept Miles's soldiers at bay. As night came and the fighting ceased, snow began to fall. In the dark and cold, the nontreaties began to bury their dead and dig foxholes and tunnels into the earth for protection. Six warriors were sent to Canada to seek help from Sitting Bull. The message did not reach Sitting Bull until too late, so the help never came. Others also fled, hoping to escape to Canada. By dawn, when Miles began his siege of their position, the ground was covered with five inches of snow. The Nez Percé had dug in as though they were prepared to fight forever, but they knew in their hearts their cause was lost.

Yellow Wolf said:

I felt the coming end. All for which we had suffered lost! Thought came of the Wallowa where I grew up. Of my own country when only Indians were there. Of tepees along the bending river. Of the blue, clear lake, wide meadows with horse and cattle herds. From the mountain forests, voices seemed calling. . . . Everything was against us. No hope! Only bondage or death! . . . Then with rifle I stood forth, saying to my heart, "Here I will die, fighting for my people and our homes!"[43]

At noon, Miles decided to ask Joseph to surrender. He was worried that Sitting Bull would send reinforcements and help the nontreaties escape. But more than that, Miles was concerned that Howard might arrive and take charge. Then if Joseph surrendered, Howard would get the credit. Miles wanted to defeat the Nez Percé and accept their surrender. So, he sent a message asking Joseph to come talk with him.

Joseph and Miles Confront One Another

The remaining chiefs held a council. Joseph wanted to talk with Miles. Looking Glass and White Bird were against it. They were afraid Joseph would surrender. If that happened, they were sure they would be hanged. But Joseph said he would just find out what Miles wanted and report back, so they agreed. No one is sure what

Nez Percé warriors meet Miles's forces head on. The fighting was fierce, bloody, and for many, to the death. As Yellow Wolf said, "Here I will die, fighting for my people and our homes!"

The Scene of Joseph's Surrender

Thomas Sutherland, a war correspondent who accompanied General Howard throughout the war, described Joseph's surrender. These excerpts are taken from a consolidation of two articles excerpted from The Flight of the Nez Percé *by Mark H. Brown.*

"As the sun was dropping to the level of the prairie . . . , Joseph came slowly riding up the hill ['on a black pony . . . dressed in a woolen shirt . . . , with a blanket of red, yellow and blue stripes around his hips, and a pair of beadless moccasins. His front hair was tied straight back from his forehead with a small strip of otter skin, . . . and the hair at the sides was braided and held back . . . by longer pieces of the same fur.'] Five of his followers walked beside him; he . . . in the center of the group. His hands were crossed on the pommel of the saddle, his head bowed upon his breast. His warriors talked in eager murmurs, he listening and making no reply. The Indian camp lay in the lengthening shadows and as the little group came up from the darkening valley into the higher light which showed their wretchedness, Joseph lifted his head, and with an impulsive gesture, straightened his arm toward General Howard, offering his rifle, as if with it he cast away all . . . hope . . . leaving his heart and his future down with his people in the dark valley.

Howard motioned Joseph to Miles and the latter received his rifle—the token of submission. ['Joseph had scarcely turned his gun over to Miles, when Indians were seen in every direction coming into our camp. Among those to surrender were many blind old men and women and lame and wounded young men, and the thought naturally arose, How could Joseph have traveled so rapidly with such maimed followers?']"

A weary Joseph surrenders, claiming, "I will fight no more forever."

Miles and Joseph said to each other. It appears Miles asked Joseph to surrender, and Joseph replied he would not. He wanted to be allowed to go home to the Wallowa Valley. The only certain thing about the meeting is its ending. Miles decided to hold Joseph prisoner, in clear violation of the flag of truce.

At the same time, however, the Nez Percé also gained a prisoner. Although no one is really sure how it happened, it appears that Lt. Lovell H. Jerome had gotten the impression the Nez Percé were going to surrender. He went to their camp to make sure they turned in all their guns. When the nontreaties realized Joseph was a prisoner, they seized Jerome. The two prisoners were exchanged on the afternoon of the third day.

By this time, the Nez Percé were hungry and freezing. As the soldiers' bullets whizzed over their heads, they lay in their foxholes and listened to their children crying. But still, Joseph said later, they were "divided about surrendering. We could have escaped from Bear Paw Mountain if we had left our wounded, old women, and children behind. We were unwilling to do this. We had never heard of a wounded Indian recovering while in the hands of white men."[44]

Late in the afternoon of the fifth day, October 4, Howard arrived. He had finally caught up with the Nez Percé. The next day, Howard and Miles sent word to Joseph. If he would surrender unconditionally, he and his people would be sent to live on the Lapwai Reservation in Idaho. He would not be allowed to return to the Wallowa Valley, but at least he would be on the traditional homeland of the Nez Percé. Joseph held a council with Looking Glass and White Bird and told them he had decided to accept these terms.

Joseph explained later:

I could not bear to see my wounded men and women suffer any longer; we had lost enough already. General Miles had promised that we might return to our own country with what stock we had left. I thought we could start again. I believed General Miles, or *I never would have surrendered*. I have heard that he has been censured [reprimanded] for making the promise to return us to Lapwai. He could not have made any other terms with me at that time. I would have held him in check until my friends came to my assistance, and then neither of the generals nor their soldiers would have ever left Bear Paw Mountain alive.[45]

Looking Glass and White Bird refused to surrender. They decided to try to escape with their people to Canada. Looking Glass never made it. Right after the council, he heard that a horseman was approaching. Thinking it might be word from Sitting Bull, he stuck his head up out of his trench to look. He was struck by a bullet in his forehead and killed.

At 2:00 P.M. on October 5, Joseph rode out to meet Howard and Miles. As he held out his rifle to Howard in a gesture of surrender, Howard smiled and motioned toward Miles. Joseph turned to Miles and handed him the rifle, thereby giving Miles the credit for the surrender. Then, as an interpreter translated and Howard's aide, Lt. Charles E. S. Wood, wrote it down, Joseph made his surrender speech.

Tell General Howard I know his heart. What he told me before, I have it in my heart. I am tired of fighting. Our chiefs are killed. Looking Glass is dead.

Yellow Wolf's Story of Joseph's Surrender

In the 1930s, Yellow Wolf told his version of Joseph's surrender at Bear Paws to historian L. V. McWhorter.

"Then Chief Joseph and other chiefs met General Miles on halfway ground. Chief Joseph and General Miles were talking good and friendly when General Howard came speaking loud, commanding words. When General Miles saw this, . . . [h]e said, 'I think soon General Howard will forget all this. I will take you to a place for this winter; then you can go to your old home.'

Chief Joseph said, 'Now we all understand these words, and we will go with General Miles. He is a head-man, and we will go with him.'

General Miles spoke to Chief Joseph, 'No more battles and blood! From this sun, we will have good time on both sides, your band and mine. We will have plenty time for sleep, for good rest. . . . '

'Same is here,' General Howard said. 'I will have time from now on, like you, to rest. The war is all quit.' He was in a better humor. General Howard spoke to Chief Joseph, 'You have your life. I am living. . . . Many of you have lost brothers, maybe more than on our side. I do not know. Do not worry any more. . . . Many brothers of yours—they are my brothers—living from the war.

'Do not worry about starving. It is plenty of food we have left from this war. Any one who needs a sack of flour, anything the people want, come get it. All is yours.'

The chiefs and officers . . . shook hands all around. The Indians lifted their hands towards the sky, where the sun was then standing. This said, 'No more battles! No more war!'"

Toohoolhoolzote is dead. The old men are all dead. It is the young men who say, "Yes" or "No." He who led the young men [Ollokot] is dead. It is cold, and we have no blankets. The little children are freezing to death. My people, some of them, have run away to the hills, and have no blankets, no food. No one knows where they are—perhaps freezing to death. I want to have time to look for my children, and see how many of them I can find. Maybe I shall find them among the dead. Hear me, my chiefs! I am tired. My heart is sick and sad. From where the sun now stands I will fight no more forever.[46]

Joseph pulled his blanket over his head. There was silence. The war was over.

The War Ends

With Joseph, 418 Nez Percé surrendered: 87 men, 184 women, and 147 children. It is estimated that 233 escaped. Of those, about 200, including White Bird, Yellow Wolf, and Joseph's daughter, made it safely to Canada. Joseph never saw his daughter again.

The Nez Percé had left their homeland in Idaho with 750 people, all their possessions, and their huge horse herds. During the almost four months of their flight, they had covered seventeen hundred miles, fighting nearly the entire way. In those battles, they had killed 180 whites and wounded 150, at the expense of 120 Nez Percé lives. In the end, those who survived were left with nothing—no horses, no possessions, no homes, no freedom. The war, which had cost the U.S. government $1,873,410 ended by making this once rich tribe dependent on the American taxpayers.

After the war, the soldiers who had fought against the Nez Percé had nothing but praise for them. For example, Miles stated that the Nez Percé "were the boldest and best marksmen of any Indians I have ever encountered. And Chief Joseph was a man of more sagacity [wisdom] and intelligence than any Indian I have ever met."[47]

Gen. William T. Sherman, commander of the U.S. Army, praised the Nez Percé in his report on the war to President Rutherford B. Hayes. Sherman wrote:

Thus has terminated one of the most extraordinary Indian wars of which there is any record. The Indians throughout displayed a courage and skill that elicited universal praise. They abstained from scalping; let captive women go free; did not commit indiscriminate murder of peaceful families, which is usual, and fought with almost scientific skill, using advance and rear guards, skirmish lines, and field fortifications.[48]

The legend that had grown up around Joseph was now solidified. The fact that Joseph had been the chief who surrendered confirmed the public's belief that he was the main war chief. The whites did not understand he had been the one who

After Joseph surrendered, President Rutherford B. Hayes heard praiseworthy accounts of Joseph's admirable conduct during the war.

Joseph Interviewed After Surrender

After he surrendered, Joseph was cooperative, friendly, and honest with the whites. He talked with war correspondent Thomas Sutherland, who dispatched the story of his interview to the San Francisco Chronicle. *It was published on November 1, 1877.*

"Physically Joseph is a splendid looking man. He is fully six feet high; in the prime of life—about 35, has a splendid face and well formed head. His forehead is high, his eyes bright yet kind, his nose finely cut, and his mouth, though determined, rather too sad looking for actual beauty. . . .

I held a long conversation with Joseph by the aid of an interpreter. . . . Poker Joe, whom I imagined at one time to be chief, was merely camp chief, directing when and where to camp, and was killed early in the Miles fight. . . . Ollicot, Joseph's brother, and Ta-hool-hool-shute were killed in rifle-pits, and Looking Glass sent to the happy hunting ground while enjoying a smoke in his tent during the fight. . . . He says he wanted to surrender at Kamiah, but he was overpowered in the council by others, especially Looking Glass, who painted the picture of the future in such rose colors that he could not resist. . . . He says that he himself committed no murders, but . . . tried to stop them, going so far as to spare Mrs. Cowan, her sister and brother, just after the Gibbon fight, when Indian women and children dead by far outnumbered the bucks. He is a temperate man and says that captured whiskey was usually at the bottom of all murders, the Indians getting almost crazy with it and utterly beyond his influence. He was glad to see General Howard, and he felt he would receive justice, and paid him the compliment of saying that it was he that broke him in spirit and strength at Clearwater."

surrendered because he was the only chief left who was willing to surrender. Furthermore, the praise from the officers who fought him made him appear legendary.

For the next twenty-seven years, Joseph's fame would help him in his single-minded goal of safeguarding the traditions and well-being of his people. But he had set himself a difficult task, much harder than he could have imagined as he sat in Miles's camp after the surrender and pondered his future.

When Joseph and his people set off with Miles to Fort Keogh, they thought they were going to spend the winter there. Their hearts were heavy but hopeful. In the spring, they thought, they would be going home.

Chapter

7 "I Have Heard Talk and Talk"

On the journey to Fort Keogh, Miles came to admire Joseph so much that he became a champion of his cause. Unfortunately, Miles could do nothing to stop what was about to happen. By the time they reached Fort Keogh, General Sherman had decided to break Miles's promise and send the nontreaties to the Quapaw Reservation

Miles became a champion of Joseph's cause and tried, unsuccessfully, to return the captive Nez Percé to Lapwai. Instead, they were sent to Indian Territory in present-day Oklahoma.

in Indian Territory, present-day Oklahoma. The whites in Idaho were still angry and bitter and did not want the nontreaties at Lapwai. The treaty Nez Percé who lived on the reservation also had doubts about being able to live peacefully with the nontreaties.

More important, however, Sherman wanted to punish Joseph and his band for disobeying the U. S. government. It is believed that Sherman once quipped: "The only good Indian is a dead Indian." He decided the nontreaties "should never again be allowed to return to Oregon or to Lapwai." They were not even allowed to rest at Fort Keogh during the bitterly cold winter.

On November 1, Miles received orders to transport his prisoners immediately to Fort Lincoln in Bismarck, North Dakota, eight hundred miles away. There were now 431 prisoners because 13 nontreaties had been captured while trying to escape to Canada. Over the next few years, many others, including Yellow Wolf, would come from Canada and be sent to join them in exile.

In Bismarck, Miles received orders to send the Nez Percé by train to Fort Leavenworth, Kansas. They would be held there as prisoners until arrangements could be made to settle them on the Quapaw Reservation. In an attempt to change these orders, Miles officially requested permission to take Joseph to Washington, D.C., to talk with President Hayes. His request was denied. Miles then had to tell Joseph he could do no more to help him.

To the nontreaties' great surprise, however, the citizens of Bismarck greeted them as heroes. "The citizens of the city, reflecting the nation's admiration for their gallantry, flocked to cheer them," wrote Alvin Josephy.

> The Indians' ragged and forlorn condition touched the whites, who gave them food in the town square. A special banquet was held for Joseph, the invitation, published in the *Bismarck Tri-Weekly Tribune* on November 21, 1877, reading:
>
> To Joseph, Head Chief of the Nez Percés.
> Sir:
>
> Desiring to show you our kind feelings and the admiration we have for your bravery and humanity, as exhibited in your recent conflict with the forces of the United States, we most cordially invite you to dine with us at the Sheridan House in this city.[49]

Leavenworth

When they reached Leavenworth on November 27, the Nez Percé were placed on an unhealthy location between a swamp and the Missouri River. One observer said the site was so miserable that it appeared to have been selected "for the express purpose of putting an end to Chief Joseph and his band."[50] According to the fort physician, half the nontreaties soon caught malaria.

Joseph's quest to regain his homeland for his people began immediately after he arrived at Leavenworth. On December 10, 1877, he and seven members of his band petitioned the government for the right to return to Idaho. If this could not be, they said, they wanted the right to select their own land at Quapaw. Sherman wrote "Disapproved" on the petition.

By July 1878, when the nontreaties were moved to Quapaw, twenty-one had died. Their new home, seven thousand desertlike acres, was almost as bad as Leavenworth. They called it Eeikish Pah, "the hot place." Without horses and cattle, they had nothing to occupy their time. Boredom killed their spirit, while many died from unsanitary conditions and lack of medication. By October, forty-seven more had died. Joseph later said, "The Great Spirit Chief who rules above seemed to be looking some other way, and did not see what was being done to my people."[51]

Under these deplorable conditions, Joseph struggled for his people's survival. He remained their guardian and spokesman. Through constant appeals for justice, he did achieve some results. E. A. Hayt, U. S. commissioner of Indian affairs, decided to inspect Joseph's camp in October 1878.

Joseph said later:

> I told him, as I told every one, that I expected General Miles's word would be carried out. He said it "could not be done; that white men now lived in my country and all the land was taken up; that, if I returned to Wallowa, I could not live in peace; that lawpapers were out against my young men who began the war, and that the Government could not protect my people." This

By 1879, Joseph's band had whittled down to 369. That year, they were moved to the Oakland Reservation near present-day Tonkawa, Oklahoma, pictured here.

talk fell like a heavy stone upon my heart. I saw that I could not gain anything by talking to him. Other law chiefs . . . [a congressional committee] came to see me and said they would help me to get a healthy country. I did not know who to believe. The white people have too many chiefs. They do not understand each other. They do not all talk alike.

The Commissioner Chief [Mr. Hayt] invited me to go with him and hunt for a better home than we have now. I like the land we found . . . [90,710 acres on the Oakland Reservation near present-day Tonkawa, Oklahoma] better than any place I have seen in that country; but it is not a healthy land. There are no mountains and rivers. The water is warm. It is not a good country for stock. I do not believe my people can live there. I am afraid they will all die. The Indians who occupy that country are dying off. I promised Chief Hayt to go there, and do the best I could until the Government got ready to make good General Miles's word. I was not satisfied, but I could not help myself.[52]

Joseph Impressed Whites

The government officials who met with Joseph were all tremendously impressed by him. His dignity, courage, wisdom, and morality were obvious, and he was a polished politician and diplomat. After talking with Joseph, Indian Inspector Gen. John O'Neill arranged a hearing for him with President Hayes in January 1879. Joseph was greeted as a celebrity in the capital. He met with Hayes and many other officials and pleaded to be returned to Idaho. When he made a speech on January 14 to a large audience of cabinet members, congressmen, and diplomats, his account of the war received nationwide attention. The conclusion of his speech is one of the most eloquent appeals for justice ever given.

Whenever the white man treats the Indian as they treat each other, then we will have no more wars. We shall all be alike—brothers of one father and one mother, with one sky above us and one country around us, and one government for all. Then the Great Spirit Chief who rules above will smile upon this land, and send rain to wash out the bloody spots made by brothers' hands from the face of the earth. For this time the Indian race are waiting and praying. I hope that no more groans of wounded men and women will ever go to the ear of the Great Spirit Chief above, and that all people may be one people.

In-mut-too-yah-lat-lat has spoken for his people.[53]

Joseph's powerful appeals stirred the American public to action. Petitions to send him back to Idaho were circulated, but the government was afraid trouble would break out if the nontreaties returned. Joseph saw he could not win that battle, but he tried another move. Since he had to settle in Oklahoma, he wanted to acquire legal title to the new land. This, he felt, would assure that his people would not be displaced again.

Therefore, before he left Washington, he filed a proposal with the Bureau of Indian Affairs. In it, he offered to trade all rights to land in Oregon and Idaho for the title to four townships of his choice in the Indian Territory, plus $250,000 and moving expenses. Although Commissioner Hayt approved the plan and submitted it to Congress, Congress never acted on it. Consequently, Joseph continued to feel he had a legal claim to the Wallowa Valley.

A Second Trip to Washington

In March, encouraged by the reaction to his first trip, Joseph again went to Washington to speak with President Hayes and other officials. The results were the same. Everyone was sympathetic, but nothing was done. This time, however, Joseph's speech was published in the April issue of the widely circulated magazine *North American Review.* It led to other interviews with newspapers and magazines. As word of the injustice done to the nontreaties began to spread, so did public support for their cause.

In June 1879, Joseph and his 369 Nez Percé were moved to their new home on the Oakland Reservation. At first, conditions were no better than before. Shelters were primitive, the weather was rainy and cold, and they received no medical attention. Almost all the children born there died, and so did many of the children who had survived the war, including Joseph's daughter born at Tolo Lake just before the war began. Gradually, however, things improved somewhat, due in part to $100,000 the government spent on the reservation. Some of the nontreaties began to farm, while others acquired small herds of cattle and horses. When three treaty Nez Percé from Idaho came to teach, the nontreaties also received some education, including instruction in the ways of Christianity for those who would listen.

Meanwhile, Joseph's trips to Washington began to pay off. Newspaper reporters visited the camp and interviewed Joseph. They kept the public alerted to his cause. The time was right for public support. By 1880, whites had settled most of the country, and most native Americans were living peacefully on reservations. Now that the native Americans were no longer a threat, many whites were beginning to question the justice of the way they had been treated.

Joseph became a symbol of the injustice done to all native Americans. He forced the white public to rethink its image of native Americans as ignorant savages to be feared, neglected, and forgotten. His

Joseph's Appeal for Justice

While visiting Washington, D.C., in 1879, Joseph was interviewed by Bishop William H. Hare, and his story appeared in the April issue of the North American Review.

"I have shaken hands with a great many friends, but there are some things I want to know which no one seems able to explain. I can not understand how the Government sends a man out to fight us, as it did General Miles, and then breaks his word. Such a Government has something wrong about it. I can not understand why so many chiefs are allowed to talk so many different ways, and promise so many different things. . . . I have heard talk and talk, but nothing is done. . . . Words do not pay for my dead people. They do not pay for my country, now overrun by white men. They do not protect my father's grave. . . . I am tired of talk that comes to nothing. . . . If the white man wants to live in peace with the Indian he can live in peace. . . . Treat all men alike. . . . Give them all an even chance to live and grow. . . . The earth is the mother of all people, and all people should have equal rights upon it. . . . I have asked some of the great white chiefs where they get their authority to say to the Indian that he shall stay in one place, while he sees white men going where they please. They can not tell me.

Let me be a free man—free to travel, free to stop, free to work, free to trade where I choose, free to choose my own teachers, free to follow the religion of my fathers, free to think and talk and act for myself—and I will obey every law, or submit to the penalty."

honesty, intelligence, and noble bearing commanded respect and admiration. He made the public feel guilty that such a worthy man had been deprived of his home in such an unfair manner.

In 1881, sensing this change in public opinion, Miles, now a general, again asked President Hayes to send the nontreaties back to Idaho. Lieutenant Wood (who had recorded Joseph's surrender speech), the Indian Rights Association, and the Presbyterian church also campaigned for his cause. "By 1883," Alvin Josephy wrote,

Joseph's future had become a national issue. Letters, telegrams, and appeals flowed into Washington, and in May of that year the government finally allowed . . . twenty-nine persons, two of them old men and the rest women and orphans, [to go] back to the Lapwai reservation.[54]

Two Versions of the Story

Finally, on July 4, 1884, Congress granted Secretary of the Interior Henry M. Teller permission to relocate the nontreaties as he saw fit. The whites' version of this relocation says that Teller decided to return the survivors of the bands headed by Looking Glass and White Bird to Lapwai but not those of Joseph's band. He did not want Joseph and his band in Idaho because the government still believed Joseph's presence there would cause problems. They were to be sent to the Colville Reservation

During their seven-year exile in Indian Territory, Joseph's band lost 101 members to famine and disease. In 1885, 149 of the remaining nontreaties accompanied Joseph to the Colville Reservation, where their living conditions improved.

in northeastern Washington where the Nespelems, San Poils, Columbias, and other small tribes lived.

Many of the Nez Percé were expected to become Christians and live like whites. This 1882 photo shows a group of Nez Percé learning to blacksmith at an Indian training school in Oregon.

According to the Nez Percé, however, officials of the Presbyterian church, which ran the Lapwai Reservation, asked all the nontreaties to make a choice. The choice was between returning to Lapwai, where they would be expected to become Christian and live like whites, and going to Colville, where they could retain their Dreamer religion and live a traditional Nez Percé life.

"When finally released from bondage [1885], brought back to this country, religion had to do with where they placed us," Yellow Wolf said.

> We believed in our own Hunyewat [God]. We had our own Ahkunkenekoo [Land Above]. Hunyewat gives us food, clothing, everything. Because we respected our religion, we were not allowed to go on the Nez Percé Reservation. When we reached Wallowa, the interpreter asked us, "Where you want to go? Lapwai and be Christian, or Colville and just be yourself?"

A bird's-eye view of the Nez Percé agency in Idaho. Of the nontreaties, 118 were permitted to rejoin their tribe at Lapwai.

No other question was asked us. . . . We answered to go to Colville Reservation.

Chief Joseph was not given choice where to go. But he had the promise that as soon as the Government got Wallowa straightened out, he could go there with his band. That was never to be.[55]

Joseph objected to the continuation of his forced exile. He felt he and his people had been punished enough. "If I could," Joseph pleaded, "I would take my heart out and hold it in my hand and let the Great Father and the white people see that there is nothing in it but kind feelings and love for Him and them."[56] But Teller would not relent. Joseph finally agreed to go to Colville, but he considered the arrangement temporary. Having succeeded this far, he was sure he would eventually be able to negotiate a return to the Wallowa Valley.

A New Home at Nespelem

On May 22, 1885, the 268 nontreaties who had survived their seven-year exile in Indian Territory boarded the train that would take them north. Only 118 of them went to Lapwai; 149 accompanied Joseph to the Colville Reservation where they established a new home at Nespelem. Even though they were in exile there also, they were now able to stay in touch with their kin in Idaho. Joseph was very popular with the non-Christian Nez Percé at Lapwai. They considered him a hero. Lapwai missionary Kate C. McBeth wrote

> For a few years at first Joseph was afraid to come down upon the Nez Percé reserve—afraid of the surround-

A Woman on the Reservation

In December 1901, ninety-year-old So-ko-mop-o described her life after the war to Henry M. Steele, who taught farming on the Colville Reservation. This excerpt is taken from With One Sky Above Us.

"After the capture and surrender of Joseph, I left and lived with the Sioux Indians. When Joseph returned from Indian Territory, I joined him. . . . In the meantime, my husband had died and his bands of horses and cattle, with other property, had entirely vanished, having been managed by unscrupulous Indians and bad white men. Many years of my life have been filled with sadness. Death has swept away my children and my two husbands and we have suffered great injustice from the government. It has taken away my old home and declines to allow me to spend the few years that I may live, in the beautiful country where I was born and spent much of my younger life. . . . I am now held as a captive and fed as a common prisoner, and for what reason I cannot understand. I have nothing to live for, my Indian pride has been crushed out of me and I fully realize my keen humiliation. I am a member of no church, I belong to no creed, but I think when I die the Great Father beyond the clouds will be kind and just to me. . . . I bear no malice or hatred toward any one and feel kindly toward all. I am an aunt of Chief Joseph and I think him a brave, honest and fearless man who fought against overwhelming odds for the defence of his home and people."

ing whites, and because of the many indictments against him—but this fear wore off. Then he visited his friends—too often for their good, for he held to his heathenism with all the tenacity with which he had clung to his beloved Wallowa Valley.[57]

Life at Nespelem was better. The land was beautiful, the climate healthy, and the supply of wildlife, roots, and berries ample. The Dreamers were allowed to worship in their own way. Gradually, the band established farms and horse and cattle herds. They leased land they did not wish to use to whites for cattle grazing. This brought in extra income. Gradually, their lives improved in their new environment.

After his wife was killed, Joseph had married two widows of slain warriors. His reply to a missionary who suggested he get rid of one was: "I fought through the war for my country and these women. You took away my country; I shall keep my

Eschewing the house provided for him at Nespelem, Joseph lived his last days in this tepee. He lived simply and was described by Erskine Wood as "considerate, kind, and respected by all."

wives."[58] Of Joseph's nine children, eight died in childhood. The daughter who had escaped to Canada died as a young adult.

Joseph's life at Nespelem was described in 1892 by Erskine Wood, the son of Lieutenant Wood, who remained good friends with Joseph. Erskine Wood twice lived with Joseph for three months. The year he was thirteen, he kept a journal. In it he wrote that horses were Joseph's main interest, and he liked to race and bet on them. He lived simply in a tepee, not in the house provided for him. He was considerate, kind, and respected by all. He saw that the young were taught tribal history, religion, and arts, but he advised them to learn both the Nez Percé traditions and the new white ways. "He took me into his tepee and into his heart and treated me as a son," Erskine Wood said as an adult. "We ate together, hunted deer together, and slept together. I can say truthfully, knowing him was the high spot of my entire life."[59]

All during his long exile at Colville, Joseph never once gave up fighting for his people's best interest. Even though his appeals to return to the Wallowa Valley were always denied, he never lost hope. In 1889,

Joseph appealed to President William McKinley for assistance in keeping whites off the Colville Reservation.

Joseph poses for a photo in 1903. The next year, he died in front of the fire in his tepee.

when the Lapwai Reservation was finally divided into family lots, the government offered to allow Joseph and his people to move there and receive allotments. They refused. They knew that accepting land at Lapwai would mean giving up forever their rights to the Wallowa Valley.

In 1897, Joseph again went to Washington, D.C. Whites were encroaching on the Colville Reservation, and he wanted assistance in keeping them off. He talked to President William McKinley, General Miles, and other officials who promised their help. Miles then took him to New York where he rode in the parade attending the dedication of Ulysses S. Grant's tomb. Joseph received a great deal of admiration

and publicity on this trip, and again Miles tried to help him in his fight to return to the Wallowa Valley. Because of Miles's efforts, the Bureau of Indian Affairs agreed to investigate Joseph's request. The result was that Joseph was allowed to visit the Wallowa Valley for the first time since the war began.

When Joseph rode into the Wallowa in August 1899, he saw a valley covered with fences and irrigation ditches. There were four small towns beside the river. He spoke at a public meeting and offered to buy some land for his people, but his offer was politely refused. He returned to Colville and continued his appeals to the government.

In June 1900, the bureau sent Inspector James McLoughlin to investigate Joseph's request. He took Joseph back to the Wallowa Valley, where Joseph paid a tearful visit to his father's grave. Then, they met with some of the valley's citizens. They told McLoughlin and Joseph that under no circumstances would they ever let the Nez Percé back into the valley. Joseph knew then his cause was hopeless, but still he did not give up.

Joseph's Death

In 1903, Joseph visited the new U.S. president, Theodore Roosevelt, in Washington, D.C., and tried unsuccessfully to win his support. His trip attracted the attention of James J. Hill, a millionaire railroad tycoon. Hill paid to bring Joseph to Seattle, Washington, in September 1904, where he spoke at a public meeting. It is impossible to know whether Hill would have succeeded in helping Joseph's cause. This was Joseph's last public appearance. On September 21,

An Opposing View of Joseph

Albert Anderson, an agent at the Colville Reservation from 1897 to 1903, made his dislike of Joseph clear in his annual reports to the commissioner of Indian affairs. Anderson was removed from his post in 1903 for misusing agency funds.

"Chief Joseph himself is not in any way a progressive Indian. . . . It is difficult to instill in his mind the fundamental principles of civilization. He lacks the stamina of a chief. . . . [He] may be applauded for . . . acts of bravery. . . . All these acts appear very flattering on the pages of history, but to know a man thoroughly is to see him daily, [and] as a progressive, public spirited Indian he is decidedly a sad failure. . . . He should be willing to elevate his people to a higher standard . . . [but] they plod along in the same rut from year to year." (1899)

"[T]he Government has erected comfortable and suitable houses for their occupancy, but none of them is ever occupied. Chief Joseph himself does not occupy the house erected on his farm, and has not resided on his farm to my certain knowledge for the past seven years. He, with his handful of unworthy followers, prefers the traditional tepee, living on the generosity of the Government and passing away their time in a filthy and licentious way of living. . . . History has been partial to Joseph in chronicling his atrocious acts. . . . The appalling wrongs done by him are crying from the bloodstained soil of Idaho for restitution." (1900)

1904, Joseph died in front of the fire in his tepee. The legend says that the reservation doctor reported he died of a broken heart.

Joseph's people buried him quietly at Colville. A monument was erected over his grave in 1905 by the Washington State Historical Society. For many years, it seemed that the legend of Joseph had been buried with him, along with the tribe's traditions. White missionaries and Indian agents taught Nez Percé children that Joseph had disgraced the tribe with his rebellion and his Dreamer religion. Christian Nez Percé,

eager to blend in with white society, regarded Joseph as a troublemaker. Most whites simply forgot him.

Some Nez Percé and a few whites, however, were determined to keep the memory of Chief Joseph alive. They formed the Chief Joseph Memorial and Historical Association, which perpetuated the legend of Joseph as a great war chief and a symbol of freedom. By the mid-1930s, their success was evident. For example, in 1936, historian Chester A. Fee wrote, "Joseph ranks with Lee, Jackson and Grant as one of the best generals this country has produced. . . . Had Joseph led thousands and had he been born . . . in a place less remote from the main currents of history, his name would resound in our ears like thunder."[60]

In 1939, the association tried to get Congress to give money for a monument and museum at Lapwai in honor of Joseph. Congress refused to act on the bill. In 1943, the association tried to get Joseph's grave moved to the Wallowa Valley. Their attempt failed. Even in death, Joseph was not allowed to return to his homeland.

A Degree of Self-Government

The people Joseph had fought so long to protect were not doing well either. The Nez Percé were too impoverished and dependent on the government to take pride in the freedom and traditions Joseph had cherished. Then, in 1948, things began to improve. With the government's approval, the tribe elected a nine-member governing group known as the Nez Percé Tribal Executive Committee (NPTEC) to manage affairs on the reservation.

With the establishment of NPTEC, it became evident that the tribe was still as divided by politics and religion as it had been in 1877. Unfortunately, this is still true today. The Nez Percé who live on the reservation are at odds with those who live off the reservation among the whites. The Christian Nez Percé are at odds with non-Christians. Those who cherish the old traditions are at odds with the more modern members of the tribe. Conflicting opinions make it difficult for the NPTEC to be effective, yet it has succeeded in making gains by following Joseph's example and

becoming politically astute. During the 1950s, for instance, the NPTEC won several claims against the U.S. government. When a traditional Nez Percé fishery was destroyed by The Dalles Dam on the Columbia River, the Nez Percé were awarded $2,800,000 in 1956. In 1959, they were awarded $3,000,000 for loss of payment for the gold taken from the reservation in the 1860s as well as $4,297,000 for underpayment for land taken in the 1863 "thief treaty." Fourteen percent of that payment went to Joseph's band for the Wallowa Valley, the land Joseph had never sold.

Then, in the 1960s and 1970s, during the height of the civil rights movement, the Nez Percé began to recapture interest in their tribal traditions and take pride in their heritage. One of the results was the 1965 establishment of the Nez Percé National Historical Park made up of twenty-four separate sites, each a part of Nez Percé history. These sites commemorate, for example, the White Bird battlefield, Fort Lapwai, Camas Meadow, the Clearwater battlefield, and the Lolo Trail.

Regaining pride, however, is a slow process. The tribe was beset with alcoholism, diabetes from the changes in their diet, suicide, and unemployment. Even though the NPTEC fought back with educational grants, law enforcement, vocational training, loans, and health services, the problems remained. In 1977, on the one hundredth anniversary of the Nez Percé War, writer William Albert Allard interviewed NPTEC member Cliff Allen. "Establishing self-pride among the young is one of the most important goals," said Allen.

It's hard to be productive if you don't have pride in what you are. Between

Joseph Poses for a Photograph

Joseph and Edward H. Latham, the physician on the Colville Reservation, did not particularly like each other. Latham often treated Joseph in a condescending manner, and Joseph's resentment of this shows in his resistance to posing for a photograph. This quote appeared with the photographs on December 25, 1904, in the Oregon Sunday Journal.

"For years I had befriended Joseph and nursed him as if he were a child when he had pneumonia, and had fed him from my cellar when he was in need of food. Knowing this I thought there would be little trouble in inducing Joseph to pose for a photograph. Joseph demurred. There is no use hurrying an Indian. Some days later I mentioned it again. He refused flatly. Winter came on. He got out of food. I gave him a sack of potatoes and mentioned the picture. He grunted. I gave him another sack of potatoes two weeks later and again I mentioned the picture. He said, 'Sometime'. . . . Then I gave him two sacks of potatoes and $5. He promised to dress in all his regalia and go to some wild spot on the river and pose for the picture. On the first pretty day, the time agreed upon for taking the picture, I appeared, camera in hand, but Joseph didn't even grunt. I appealed to his squaws. One of them began jabbering and going for him in true squaw fashion. I heard her mention the potatoes several times over. Then he got up and said 'All right,' and the pictures here given was the result."

the ages of 16 and 25 many Indians find themselves suspended between two worlds. They're educated to be white, but their spirit calls out to be what they are—Indians. For years we have been taught that the only way to succeed is to be white. We must reverse that kind of education and teach Indians to be Indians. Along with skills we must teach customs, traditions, languages, and treaties. Few Indians *or* whites know much about treaties this country has made. They should be taught in all public schools.[61]

Current Tribal Problems

All these problems still exist today, and it is difficult to tell if Joseph's long struggle had any lasting influence on the life of his tribe. There are now about three thousand Nez Percé, most of whom live on or near the Lapwai Reservation. Between three and four hundred live at Nespelem, and a few still live in Canada. Some of them practice many of the traditions Joseph upheld. There are still Dreamers, now called Long House People, in the tribe. They still

The establishment of the Nez Percé National Historical Park in 1965 marked a renewed interest in Nez Percé tribal traditions and heritage.

breed and race horses, dig roots, hunt, and fish. The values Joseph stood for, such as honesty, perseverance, community involvement, and respect for elders, are very much alive. Certainly, many Nez Percé families would not be here today if Joseph had not protected their forefathers.

The Nez Percé do not like to talk to whites about Joseph and the war. They resent the whites' legend of Joseph because it falsifies their culture and history. Also, the war is painful for them to recall, and because of the numerous divisions in the tribe, there are a number of different opinions about everything, including Joseph. No tribal member is willing or able to state how the tribe feels about Joseph's importance. Moreover, they still distrust whites for many understandable reasons.

Joe Redthunder, leading elder of the Nez Percé on the Colville Reservation, told Allard in 1977:

There are some of us who know the stories of those days. We are often asked to tell them. Whites come around asking questions, but we don't tell them anything. Sometimes they offer money, and friends say, "Oh, they're white people—they won't know the difference—tell them anything and get the money." But that's not right. No, we will tell those stories to our children when the time is right. When we think they are capable of taking care of it—we

In the Wallowa Valley, throngs of whites fill a hillside to honor a monument memorializing Chief Joseph.

Joseph Praised in Death

On September 24, 1904, Joseph's obituary appeared in the New York Sun.

"With the death of Chief Joseph, . . . the United States has lost its most celebrated Indian. . . . He was the last of the great warrior chiefs. . . . [F]ollowed with constant devotion by his dwindling people, Chief Joseph was the last Indian leader who dared to put up a real fight against civilization; and in his desperate Waterloo he put up a fight that gave Gen. Nelson A. Miles and Gen. O. O. Howard all they could do to nab him and crush him till he grimly buried the hatchet. . . . When he took up the cause of his little band again it was with the diplomacy of a vanquished man. . . .

The chief's first visit to New York [was] in 1897. . . . While in New York . . . the big chief stayed at the Astor House. . . . He wore his enormous headdress . . . , and it caused more craning of . . . necks than anything else about him. Joseph, however, . . . had his own opinion about some New York [hats], though he didn't say anything to indicate this until one afternoon in an Indian exhibition camp in South Brooklyn. . . .

Here he was visited by a young woman who was dressed to impress and had store of . . . questions to ask.

'Did you ever scalp anybody?' she inquired. Chief Joseph pondered a moment and then turned to the interpreter. 'Tell her,' he said, pointing at the combination aviary and garden [a hat decorated with birds and flowers] on her head, 'that I have nothing in my collection as fine as that.' . . .

Chief Joseph was famous for his face and figure. He was tall, straight as an arrow and wonderfully handsome. . . . He never spoke a word of English, but some of his sayings, translated, have become famous. He used to say: 'Look twice at a two-faced man'; 'Cursed be the hand that scalps the reputation of the dead'; 'Big name often stands on small legs'; 'Finest fur may cover toughest meat.'"

will give the history to our children. That is the Indian way.[62]

Dr. Steven Evans, associate professor of Western American history, and Dr. Allan Marshall, professor of anthropology, both at Lewis-Clark State College in Lewiston, Idaho, work with the Nez Percé in Idaho. Evans is married to a tribal member. They both agree that Joseph is important today as a symbol of tribal pride. Evans points out as evidence the numerous uses of Joseph's name—a town in Oregon named Joseph, the Chief Joseph Dam in Washington, the Chief Joseph's and Warriors' Memorial Powwow in Idaho, a three-day

Said Erskine Wood of the forgiving Joseph: "There was no hatred in his soul in spite of the wrongs our race had done him."

A Nez Percé woman in tribal costume participates in a parade commemorating the Nez Percé.

Chief Joseph Days rodeo in the Wallowa Valley, and numerous enterprises with names like Chief Joseph Optical Supplies.

Marshall says, "The Nez Percé consider Joseph a man of great substance, an example of the struggle needed if a person is to live his life as he sees fit. But Joseph is also a two-edged sword that can be used to beat the Nez Percé with today. That makes some of them ambivalent about him." That is so, he explains, because whites all over the world consider Joseph so noble, wise, and self-sacrificing that they often accuse the Nez Percé of not living up to his example.

Although the tribe treasures Joseph's memory, both Evans and Marshall say he is only one of the so-called patriot chiefs who are admired and honored for their role in the struggle for freedom. The Nez Percé also hold White Bird, Toohoolhoolzote, Looking Glass, and others in high esteem because they feel the struggle was a collective effort. Together, they feel, these forefathers bequeathed them a proud heritage.

As important as Joseph was and is to the Nez Percé, in the end, he may be of primary importance in what he symbolizes to the whites. Joseph's words and actions helped bring about the recognition that native Americans were not savages who deserved to be destroyed. With that recognition came the understanding that their cultures and histories should be preserved as a rich part of American heritage. Perhaps the main reason Joseph was able to make whites understand this is because they felt he forgave them and was willing to work with them to right the injustice. "There was no hatred in his soul in spite of the wrongs our race had done him," said Erskine Wood at the dedication of Chief Joseph Dam. "He was a man of true magnanimity." [63]

Notes

Chapter 1: "I Will Tell You How the Indian Sees Things"

1. Reuben Golden Thwaites, ed., *Original Journals of the Lewis and Clark Expedition.* New York: Dodd, Mead, 1904.
2. Paul Allen, Esq., ed., *The Expedition of Lewis and Clark.* Vol. 2, *Meriwether Lewis*, March of America Facsimile Series, no. 56. Ann Arbor, MI: University Microfilms, 1966.
3. Alvin M. Josephy Jr., *The Nez Percé Indians and the Opening of the Northwest.* New Haven: Yale University Press, 1971.
4. Washington Irving, *Adventures of Captain Bonneville.* Portland, OR: Binfords & Mort, n.d. Possible 1959 reprint.
5. Chief Joseph, "An Indian's View of Indian Affairs," *North American Review*, April 1879.

Chapter 2: "My Father Never Sold Our Land"

6. Lawrence Kip, *Indian Council at Walla Walla 1897.* Facsimile reproduction. Seattle, WA: Shorey Publications, 1971.
7. Report of the adjutant general of Oregon. 1865–66.
8. Chief Joseph, *North American Review.*
9. Chief Joseph, *North American Review.*
10. Chief Joseph, *North American Review.*
11. Chief Joseph, *North American Review.*
12. Chief Joseph, *North American Review.*
13. J. B. Monteith, in a letter to E. P. Smith. August 27, 1872. Lapwai File.
14. Chief Joseph, *North American Review.*
15. Oliver O. Howard, *Nez Percé Joseph.* Boston: Lee & Shepard, 1881.

Chapter 3: "My Heart Was Hurt"

16. Oliver O. Howard, *Annual Report to the United States War Department*, 1875.
17. Henry Clay Wood, *Supplementary to the Report on the Treaty Status of Young Joseph.* Portland, OR: Assistant Adjutant General's Office, 1876.
18. Chief Joseph, *North American Review.*
19. Josephy, *The Nez Percé Indians and the Opening of the Northwest.*
20. Josephy, *The Nez Percé Indians and the Opening of the Northwest.*
21. Chief Joseph, *North American Review.*
22. Josephy, *The Nez Percé Indians and the Opening of the Northwest.*

Chapter 4: "I Would Have Taken My People to Buffalo Country Without Fighting"

23. Harvey Chalmers II, *The Last Stand of the Nez Percé.* New York: Twayne, 1962.
24. Chief Joseph, *North American Review.*
25. Howard, *Nez Percé Joseph.*
26. Chalmers, *The Last Stand of the Nez Percé.*
27. Chalmers, *The Last Stand of the Nez Percé.*

Chapter 5: "We Understood There Was to Be No More War"

28. Chief Joseph, *North American Review.*
29. Chief Joseph, *North American Review.*
30. John Gibbon, *Report of the Battle of Big Hole, with the List of Killed and Wounded.* Document no. 3595DD 1877, National Archives.
31. Chief Joseph, *North American Review.*
32. John Gibbon, "The Battle of the Big Hole," *Harper's Weekly*, December 28, 1895.

33. Chalmers, *The Last Stand of the Nez Percé*.

34. Chalmers, *The Last Stand of the Nez Percé*.

35. Tom Baker, *Helena* (Montana) *Daily Independent*, June 15, 1896.

36. Heister D. Guie and L. V. McWhorter, eds., *Adventures in Geyser Land*. Caldwell, ID: The Caxton Printers, 1935.

37. S. G. Fisher, *Chief of Scouts to General Howard During the Nez Percé Campaign*. Helena, MT: State Publishing Co., 1896.

Chapter 6: "I Will Fight No More Forever"

38. Oliver O. Howard, *Supplementary Report*, Sturgis to Howard, September 15, 1877. Document no. 6137-77, National Archives.

39. Chalmers, *The Last Stand of the Nez Percé*.

40. *New Northwest*. Deer Lodge, MT: October 12, 1877.

41. L. V. McWhorter, *Hear Me, My Chiefs*. Caldwell, ID: The Caxton Printers, 1952.

42. Chief Joseph, *North American Review*.

43. Chalmers, *The Last Stand of the Nez Percé*.

44. Chief Joseph, *North American Review*.

45. Chief Joseph, *North American Review*.

46. Josephy, *The Nez Percé Indians and the Opening of the Northwest*.

47. Nelson A. Miles, *Serving the Republic*. New York: Harper & Brothers, 1911.

48. Merrill D. Beal, *I Will Fight No More Forever*. Seattle: University of Washington Press, 1985.

Chapter 7: "I Have Heard Talk and Talk"

49. Josephy, *The Nez Percé Indians and the Opening of the Northwest*.

50. McWhorter, *Hear Me, My Chiefs*.

51. Chief Joseph, *North American Review*.

52. Chief Joseph, *North American Review*.

53. Chief Joseph, *North American Review*.

54. Josephy, *The Nez Percé Indians and the Opening of the Northwest*.

55. Chalmers, *The Last Stand of the Nez Percé*.

56. Beal, *I Will Fight No More Forever*.

57. Kate C. McBeth, *The Nez Percé Since Lewis and Clark*. New York: F. H. Revell, 1908.

58. Chester A. Fee, *Chief Joseph: The Biography of a Great Indian*. New York: Wilson-Erickson, 1936.

59. Erskine Wood, *Wenatchee* (Washington) *Daily World*, June 13, 1956.

60. Fee, *Chief Joseph: The Biography of a Great Indian*.

61. William Albert Allard, "Chief Joseph," *National Geographic*, March 1977.

62. Allard, *National Geographic*.

63. Beal, *I Will Fight No More Forever*.

For Further Reading

William Albert Allard, "Chief Joseph," *National Geographic,* March 1977. Combines a discussion of the sites of the Nez Percé National Historical Park with the history that took place on them; also contains interviews with members of the tribe and local whites. Contains beautiful photographs.

Harvey Chalmers II, *The Last Stand of the Nez Percé.* New York: Twayne, 1962. An eyewitness account of the war by Yellow Wolf juxtaposed with a historical account of the war from the whites' viewpoint.

"Chief Joseph," *Cobblestone: The History Magazine for Young People,* September 1990. Entire issue is devoted to Chief Joseph and the Nez Percé, with sections on history, crafts, and people close to Joseph.

Michael Gibson, *The American Indians: From Colonial Times to the Present.* Hove, England: Wayland, 1974. An overview of the conflict between native Americans and whites from first contacts to the present, using numerous original quotes and photographs.

Jason Hook, *Chief Joseph: Guardian of the Nez Percé.* New York: Sterling, 1989. A historical account of the Nez Percé that focuses on Chief Joseph and his actions to protect and serve his people.

Oliver LaFarge, revised by Alvin M. Josephy Jr., *A Pictorial History of the American Indian.* New York: Bonanza Books, 1974. An overview of many native American tribes that is loaded with photographs.

L. V. McWhorter, *Hear Me, My Chiefs.* Caldwell, ID: The Caxton Printers, 1952. A compilation of the tribe's story from their oral traditions and memories after McWhorter spent years talking with the Nez Percé and studying their history and traditions.

Marian T. Place, *Retreat to the Bear Paw.* New York: Four Winds Press, 1969. An easy-to-read history of the Nez Percé from prehistoric times to the 1960s and the story of their flight to freedom.

Works Consulted

Books

Paul Allen, Esq., ed., *The Expedition of Lewis and Clark,* Vol. 2, *Meriwether Lewis.* Philadelphia: Bradford & Inskeep, 1814. Reprint. March of America Facsimile Series, no. 56. Ann Arbor, MI: University Microfilms, 1966. Contains the original journals, including entries concerning the Nez Percé, kept by Lewis during the Lewis and Clark expedition of 1804–06.

The American Heritage Book of Indians. New York: American Heritage/Bonanza Books, 1982. A well-illustrated, overview of the history of native Americans with an introduction by President John F. Kennedy.

Merrill D. Beal, *I Will Fight No More Forever.* Seattle: University of Washington Press, 1985. A clear, concise, well-documented history of the contacts and conflicts between the Nez Percé and the whites; contains many original sources and anecdotes.

Cyrus Townsend Brady, *Northwestern Fights and Fighters.* Reprint. Williamstown, MA: Corner House Publishers, 1974. Written in turn-of-the-century style, this account of several native American chiefs and wars, including Joseph and the flight of the Nez Percé, is most noteworthy for its contemporary sources.

Mark H. Brown, *The Flight of the Nez Percé.* New York: G. P. Putnam's Sons, 1967. The history and flight of the Nez Percé are well documented by original sources in this easy-to-read book.

Chester A. Fee, *Chief Joseph: The Biography of a Great Indian.* New York: Wilson-Erickson, 1936. Now an interesting period piece, this work perpetuates the myth of Chief Joseph as a great war chief.

Jane E. Gay, *With the Nez Percé: Alice Fletcher in the Field, 1889–92.* Lincoln: University of Nebraska Press, 1981. From 1889 to 1892, Jane Gay lived on the Lapwai Reservation with Alice Fletcher, who was responsible for parceling out allotments of land to the Nez Percé. This book contains letters written by Gay describing her time on the reservation, along with a number of her photographs of the Nez Percé.

M. Gidley, *Kopet.* Seattle: University of Washington Press, 1981. *Kopet,* meaning "that is all," is the way the Nez Percé ended their speeches. The book portrays Joseph through the eyes of several whites who became involved with him at Nespelem and contains many original letters and speeches, as well as photographs.

M. Gidley, *With One Sky Above Us: Life on an Indian Reservation at the Turn of the Century.* New York: G. P. Putnam's Sons, 1979. A description of life at Nespelem around 1900, using many original sources and photographs; focuses on Joseph and the other native Americans who lived on the reservation with him.

Oliver O. Howard, *Nez Percé Joseph.* Boston: Lee & Shepard, 1881. Howard justifies his handling of the campaign against the Nez Percé in the 1877 war and presents Joseph as a native American Napoleon.

Washington Irving, *Adventures of Captain Bonneville.* Portland, OR: Binfords & Mort, n.d. Possible 1959 reprint. Originally published in 1904. Irving interviewed Bonneville and wrote this story of his adventures in the Oregon Country in the 1830s. Bonneville admired the Nez Percé and was the first American citizen to meet Joseph's father and band.

Alvin M. Josephy Jr., *The Nez Percé Indians and the Opening of the Northwest*. New Haven: Yale University Press, 1971. Josephy, although criticized for errors in this book, wrote a scholarly, detailed history of the Nez Percé and their conflicts with the whites; well documented with original sources.

Annette Rosenstiel, *Red and White: Indian Views of the White Man, 1492–1982*. New York: Universe Books, 1983. Contains many speeches and original documents that show the way native Americans, including Chief Joseph, felt about whites from the sixteenth century into the twentieth century.

Reuben Golden Thwaites, ed., *Original Journals of the Lewis and Clark Expedition*. New York: Dodd, Mead, 1904. Reprint. New York, 1959. Contains the original journals kept by both Meriwether Lewis and William Clark during their 1804–06 expedition; includes entries concerning the Nez Percé.

U.S. Department of the Interior, *Nez Percé Country: Official National Park Handbook*. Washington, D.C.: National Park Service Division of Publications, 1983. Written by Alvin Josephy, who corrected errors contained in his book *The Nez Percé Indians and the Opening of the Northwest;* contains a concise history of the Nez Percé and their conflicts with the whites, as well as a guide to the Nez Percé National Historical Park.

Deward E. Walker Jr., *Conflict and Schism in Nez Percé Acculturation*. Seattle: Washington State University Press, 1968. A scholarly work that examines the various factions within the Nez Percé tribe and how conflicts between these groups have affected the tribe's culture.

Robert Penn Warren, *Chief Joseph of the Nez Percé*. New York: Random House, 1983. A long, narrative poem that praises Chief Joseph and his life's work.

Jon Manchip White, *Everyday Life of the North American Indian*. New York: Holmes & Meier, 1979. A general guide to the lives of native Americans that contains a look at many tribes, including the Nez Percé, plus a section on the formation and maintenance of reservations from the beginning to the present.

Periodicals

Chief Joseph, "An Indian's View of Indian Affairs," *North American Review,* April 1879. Joseph's own story of his tribe's traditions and its conflicts with whites, as well as an eloquent plea for justice.

Oliver O. Howard, "The True Story of the Wallowa Campaign," *North American Review,* July 1879. After Joseph's interview was published in this magazine, Howard wrote this article to tell his version of the council he held with Joseph in May 1877.

Personal Conversations

Dr. Steven Evans, associate professor of Western American history, Lewis-Clark State College, Lewiston, Idaho.

Dr. Allan Marshall, professor of anthropology, Lewis-Clark State College, Lewiston, Idaho.

Index

Picture Credits

Cover photo by Library of Congress

The Bettmann Archive, 41, 82

Historical Pictures/Stock Montage, 31, 52 (bottom), 74 (both), 77

Historical Photographs Collections, Washington State University Libraries, 32, neg. #70-0251; 59 (top), neg. #78-152; 61, neg. #82-002; 62 (top), neg. #80-037; 65 (top), neg. #70-0235; 65 (bottom), neg. #82-011; 66, neg. #70-0256; 72, neg. #70-0238; 75, neg. #82-014

Library of Congress, 12, 17 (both), 19, 27, 33, 37, 38, 43 (bottom), 44, 50, 80, 90 (bottom), 91

Michael Maydak, 53, 57, 64, 70, 76

Montana Historical Society, Helena, 47 (bottom), 52 (top)

National Archives, 26, 35, 39, 43 (top), 87 (bottom), 88

National Museum of American Art, Washington, DC/Art Resource, NY, 21 (both)

National Museum of the American Indian, Smithsonian Institution, 84

National Park Service, Nez Percé National Historical Park, 95 (top), 97 (bottom)

Oregon Historical Society, 11, 13, 15, 16, 20, 23, 24, 25 (both), 28 (top), 29, 36, 46, 47 (top), 51, 55, 87 (top), 90 (top), 95 (bottom), 97 (top)

Smithsonian Institution, 62 (bottom)

Washington State Historical Society, Tacoma, Washington, 22, 28 (bottom), 30

About the Author

Lois Warburton earned her master's degree in education at Clark University in Worcester, Massachusetts. Her previous published works include nonfiction articles, magazine columns, short stories, and poetry. In 1990, she retired from her own word processing, writing, and editing business to travel and write books. This is her sixth book for Lucent Books.